CREATIVE ENCOUNTERS

A NEW APPROACH TO SPIRITUAL GROWTH
FOR THE RECOVERING COMMUNITY

DR. LEASA ROSE HOGAN

CONTENTS

ABSTRACT

As believers are set free from substance abuse, the church often lacks the resources needed to support the renewal and spiritual formation of those in recovery. These individuals frequently struggle with unresolved trauma, life-controlling issues, entrenched mindsets, guilt, shame, and broken relationships, all of which can impede their spiritual formation and Kingdom impact. To address this need, this book, *Creative Encounters: A New Approach to Spiritual Growth for the Recovering Community*, moves beyond traditional Bible studies, devotionals, and workbooks to integrate creative and kinesthetic learning methods for spiritual formation and healing. Designed for both individuals in recovery and the servant-leaders who support them, this resource bridges the gaps between discipleship programs, rehabilitation, and deep-seated spiritual needs.

Because restoration occurs through scriptural application, healthy community, and direct spiritual encounters, the book emphasizes the diverse ways individuals interact with God and how they listen and learn from Him. Each chapter features a biblical character or spiritual theme for study and personal application and then provides a creative encounter to help readers artistically express what God is revealing to them. The artwork produced in the creative encounter serves as tangible reminders of their experience with the Holy Spirit. By facilitating hands-on engagement with Scripture, the book empowers readers to dismantle old mindsets and embrace lasting lifestyle changes to achieve holistic restoration and spiritual growth within the local church.

Introduction

My struggle with addiction stemmed from a nightmare-like horseback ride on a barn-sour horse. The resulting back injury altered my ability to perform regular activities, but I found a workaround by using opioids. With opioids, I had super-powers. I could clean the house, play with the kids, and leap buildings in a single bound. Drugs allowed me to live a regular life despite the limits from the injury. I overrode the pain with substance use. Drugs were my workaround solution.

Pain is an indicator that something is wrong in the body, the spirit, or the mind. I didn't want to pay attention to this slow-your-roll sign and would rather control and manipulate my body through drugs. When the pain medication supply ended, I found drugs on the street. I visited sketchy areas and dark parking lots. Our boys (our daughter was born later) were witnesses to my strange behaviors while I was loaded and while I was jonesing.[1] I still need to be aware of control and selfishness.

After surgery, I eventually healed both physically and

spiritually. I learned to accept my limitations. I had difficulty functioning without drugs. I didn't cook, clean, grocery shop, or even engage in marital intimacy as I labored for sobriety. My dear husband encouraged me to rest and live within the boundaries of my fragile body.

I was a young, white, middle-class mother of two, and I was an addict. I have reflected on the toll that drug addiction took on my relationships. The greatest costs were my relationship with God, my husband, and my children. Children of drug users face lasting effects that distort their identities, leaving deep wounds. Forgiveness of myself has been hard-fought.

As part of the recovery community, I have looked for big events, programs, and hype to sustain and transform me. I have spent energy chasing the God-high, the next dopamine rush, and the elusive twelve steps to God, all while maintaining sober living. However, being set free from drug addiction and substance abuse does not equal a renewed mind or sanctified heart. Layers of confusion created from lies and traumatic events result in identity issues and a screwed-up perspective of God. By turning to idols to satiate my need for dignity, security, love, and value, I racked up more layers that kept me from God. The good news is that Jesus peels off the layers. He did this for me, and He can do it for you.

As you read this book, I assume that Jesus is your Savior and that you or someone you love is in recovery. I assume you desire an authentic relationship with God. But it's important to remember that sober living does not mean we have spiritual health. Getting clean, kicking the habit, and staying on the wagon is a step toward health, but there's more. We must intentionally seek transformation for holistic health. Spiritual formation calls us to take a closer look at our mindsets, habits, and perspectives. The Holy Spirit is with you on the journey to complete health.

Spiritual formation begins with a correct view of God. Humanity's perspective of God must be revised to reflect the truth found in the Bible. God created humans in His image. The *imago Dei* includes the whole of a person's being—their spirit, soul, mind, emotions, and body. Dallas Willard celebrates the use of imagery in Scripture to establish a restorative relationship with Jesus Christ and replace sin with His righteousness, an important role in spiritual formation: "The process of spiritual formation in Christ is one of progressively replacing our destructive images and ideas with images and ideas that filled the mind of Jesus himself."[2] For Christians, the intentional exchange results in wholeness as Jesus restores people to the Father, mainly through the growth of biblical truth. Spiritual formation closes the gap between one's current sinful state and a regenerated one, from the old self to the new self. This leads to a new attitude towards life that aligns with the Word of God and promotes holistic health.

Any intervention aimed at personal growth and development must be practical, supportive, and applicable to daily life. This involves breaking down larger goals into smaller, more manageable steps and taking consistent action towards them. It also means seeking support from mentors, peers, or professional coaches who can provide guidance, encouragement, and accountability.

An obstacle frequently arising in recovery education is the accommodation of distinct learning modalities and varying cognitive abilities. Due to the nature of drug and alcohol abuse, thinking, reasoning, and social processes are often hindered. It is essential for addiction recovery resources to recognize this diversity and develop Spirit-inspired teaching strategies that facilitate a productive learning environment. This resource does that.

Using studies of biblical characters, we will assign an image to each one and then apply these images to our spiritual formation. These practices will bring you closer to the Father, Son, and Holy Spirit. It doesn't use fog machines, catchy worship music, or even free coffee. Instead, and most importantly, it uses Scripture, a mirror, some creative space, and supplies. As we look at these people in the Bible, we will see how they relate to our lives and expect God to transform us. Then—here's the fun part—we will get together with the Holy Spirit and creatively express the truths we've learned. We will paint, glue, and even rip up old, abandoned hymnals! I can hear all the creatives getting excited and exclaiming, "Yes, please!" And I can hear all the perfectionists in their worry, saying, "Please don't make me draw."

Either way, take a deep breath and see what God has in store for you.

CHAPTER 1: ADMITTING THE ISSUES

Introduction

Let's jump right into the serious issues. The character of God has been attacked, the identity of humankind has been assaulted, and idolatry is rampant. Trauma has not been adequately addressed, leaving a plethora of lies running free and destroying lives. Your perspective shapes your attitude, which in turn influences your outlook on life. Behaviors flow from that attitude, with consequences that lead to specific outcomes. Perspective, attitude, behavior, consequences, and outcome—we filter our world through these layers. Our perspective of God, self, and others must be founded on the revealed Word of God. Our thinking must be cleared of influences, lies, and strongholds so that we fully become image bearers of God. As the *imago Dei*, we walk in grace by faith and are able to completely love ourselves and others.

As A. W. Tozer notes, our perspective of God overshadows our operating framework: "What comes into our minds when we think about God is the most important thing to us."[3] Tozer was rightly convinced that a correct perspective on God is the starting point for spiritual wholeness. He goes on to describe how the brokenness of morals comes from an internal brokenness of the image of God.

Maligned Character of God

As time has passed, people have lost their awe and wonder of God. We have exchanged the all-powerful One for a lesser, milder god of our own making, a god that we can manage, be friends with, and take out now and then when things get tough, when we need an extra boost of confidence or support. We prefer a god who doesn't spoil our plans for fun. We want a god who can neatly fit into our planner and schedule, one who doesn't demand too much of us or judge us.

However, there is only one true God, and He overwhelms us with His presence. He is larger than life and is like the air that our lungs need. He attends to our details, like the black dots on a ladybug and every wisp of every feather on every bird. Even though He lovingly attends to us, it doesn't mean we are in relationship with Him, nor does it mean that, even if we are in a relationship with Him, we are fully submitted to Him.

The reason why is that the fall of humankind damaged our relationship with God. In the creation account, God established human value, but the fall of Adam and Eve damaged our relationship with God and fractured our identity. The sin nature includes consequences of guilt, shame, idolatry, and various forms of indulgences, such as idol worship. Humanity's brokenness is healed only through a covenant relationship with Jesus Christ. Covenants found throughout the Word of God ultimately point to the New Covenant, through which Jesus rescued and restored humanity.

Identity, The Beginning of a Relationship

As described in Genesis 1 and 2, God began His relationship with humankind as He established the foundation of the world. His interactions with Adam and Eve in the Garden of Eden reveal His nature and character. Gordon Wenham points out that the beginning of the relationship between God and people, as described in Genesis, introduces the covenant-making Creator: "Genesis is not interested in events for their own sake but for what they disclose about the nature of God and His purposes."[4] God wanted obedience, communication, transparency, and fellowship. His revealed nature is loving, faithful, and holy. Unhindered intimacy shared between the Father and humankind was unique; however, disobedience marred humanity and severed the relationship with the Lord. Sandra Richter notes the effects of the Fall on humanity. The long-lasting effects of which are still felt today. She observes: "With the Fall, humanity loses their identity as God's people, their place in his paradise and their access to his presence. Intimacy with God, which was the essence of humanity's existence, is shattered."[5]

Made in His Image

The original connection with God featured relationship and intimacy between God and humanity. A relationship is defined as "the state or fact of being related; the way in which two things are connected; a connection, an association. Also: kinship."[6] God desires relationship and connection with His creation just as He has with the Son, the Spirit, and the hosts of heaven. Genesis 1:26 states, "Let us make man in our image, after our likeness." Theologians have differing views on what "our" means in this passage. John Skinner notes that, historically, the Church believed that the word is an "allusion to the Trinity," but Skinner explains that such a "doctrine is entirely unknown to the Old Testament and cannot be implied here."[7] It is unclear if God (*'ĕlōhîm*) discusses these plans with the Spirit and the Son, or possibly a divine council. Skinner asserts that God is "taking counsel with divine beings other than Himself, [namely] the angels or host of heaven."[8] All possibilities lead to God as the supreme and primary authority.

However, Psalm 103:20–21 contradicts this perspective: "Bless the Lord, you His angels, who are mighty, and do His commands … you servants who do His pleasure." According to Brannon Ellis, this Scripture implies that angels are not creative agents, they are merely witnesses and do the bidding work of God: "Angels are intelligent, moral, and spiritual beings created by God who worship him and carry out his will."[9] Regardless of one's opinion, the text reveals that God's character is clearly relational and interpersonal, whether He is interacting with the Holy Spirit and the Son, or heavenly hosts and angels.

Genesis 1:26 also refers to God making humankind in His image. "Image" translates from the Hebrew word *ṣelem*, which "indicates a likeness or representation resembling something or someone."[10] According to Mark Biddle et al. God created humankind in His likeness to bear His image, His semblance, and other qualities. Sandra Richter argues that God created his own image in us, an idol of sorts, and does not want any other to be created in our place.

It may surprise you to learn that ṣelem (with its cognates) is the standard ancient Near Eastern word for "idol." When a polytheist from the ancient world set out to make an earthly representative of their deity (understood as the incarnation of that which could not be fully incarnated, a lifeless object that must be animated by the deity), that polytheist fashioned a ṣelem. When the language of Genesis 1:26-27 is combined with the images of Genesis 2:7, we see that Yahweh is presenting himself to us as a divine craftsman, who is making an idol of/for himself, which he himself must animate. And that idol is us. Within the worldview of the ancient Near East the message here is clear: we are the nearest representation of Yahweh that exists.[11]

God created humankind in His likeness; therefore, humans also have the capacity for compassion and goodness. There exists the belief that the seed of godly identity was deposited in humankind at creation. Allen C. Meyers agrees, adding that this seed of identity remains, even after the Fall: "Most interpreters agree that the image of God has been radically distorted by sin—faculties dimmed, relations broken, dominion became tyranny—yet not wholly lost."[12] Laird R. Harris et al. offers a different perspective on sin's effects on the image of God, arguing that sin damages it: "God's image obviously does not consist in man's body which was formed from earthly matter, but in his spiritual, intellectual, moral likeness to God from whom his animating breath came. … This spiritual aspect of man has been damaged by the fall and is daily tarnished by sin."[13] Harris agrees that the work done on Calvary is the only way for restoration, and, indeed, the *imago Dei* is ultimately restored through the New Covenant, Jesus Christ.

All of creation, including plant life, animal life, ocean life, land masses, and the stars and planets, was produced by the words of God, yet humankind was uniquely formed by His hands, and He breathed His breath into humanity. Bria Burns suggests that this difference in creation carries profound meaning: "God makes Adam and Eve with his hands rather than his words, and he charges them with the care of the rest of creation. When God called his creation 'very good,' he implied that mankind, his highest creation, contained no flaws: they possessed 'original integrity.'"[14]

Loss of Relationship but Still in His Image

Still, sin has robbed humanity of its God-given authority.

This loss of relationship with the Father created a sense of brokenness, yet our identity remains anchored in the Word of God. Paul reminds believers that "we are His workmanship, created in Christ Jesus for good works, which God prepared beforehand, so that we should walk in them" (Eph 2:10). Identity was bestowed upon humankind through the breath of God. Authority over creation was also assigned at creation. Human authority must not be minimized, even as culture has discounted much of scriptural authority through the promotion of green programs, environmental practices, and conservation efforts. God has assigned humankind value, dignity, authority, and a unique identity.

Zachary Lycans celebrates the fact that life and value are allocated at the very beginning of humankind: "When breath entered into the man, he was assigned unique individuality. This union of the physical and spiritual, which distinguished humanity from the rest of creation, was entirely dependent upon the relational intimacy between humanity and its Creator."[15] God crowns His creation with a loving relationship and gives them a place of prominence and authority on the earth. In writing about the *imago Dei,* Jerry Johnson relates humanity's ruling with God: "Ancient pagan [religions believe] that only ruling kings enjoyed royal standing before the gods and men, as evidenced by their dominion which they presumed to exercise on behalf of their deities."[16] The pagan view contradicts the Bible's teaching on the dignity and authority of humankind. Johnson asserts that Genesis 1:28 overrides other verses: "By virtue of mankind's ruling over the rest of God's creatures and earth, every member of the human race somehow represents and reflects the sovereign Lord of creation." In view of Psalm 8, the image of God is what He does; the image is not a possession but a verb. As imagers of God, humankind rules over the works of God's hands. The search for identity comes to fulfillment once Jesus is made Lord and Savior of one's life. Jesus restores identity, authority, and relationship with God.

The Dignity of God's Creation

Various faith traditions, including the Catholic Church, promote the dignity of humankind through robust compassion ministries. The social teaching from Pope Leo XIII in 1891 highlights the inherent dignity of humankind regardless of social or economic status: "Social teaching also regards dignity as unconditional, in no way dependent upon who people are or what they do, and applying to all alike: saints and sinners, Christians and non-Christians, rich and poor, adults and children, the wise and those who suffer from severe cognitive impairment, and so on."[17] This teaching rightly contradicts the claims of evolutionists, who fail to recognize the identity, uniqueness, value, and esteem of humanity that the creation account conveys.

Intelligent design, according to Walter A. Elwell and Philip Wesley Comfort, is supported in Scripture: "Genesis 2:7 states unambiguously that man became a living being; the Bible does not present the view that a previously living creature developed into a human, nor does it suggest that the image of God evolved from a lower form of life."[18] Myths and evolutionary science lies are poured into culture through the media, legal systems, and academia. The image of God must be celebrated, taught, and instilled in the hearts of precious children by Christian parents. Moses relayed the commandment to teach God's Word "to your children, talking about them when you sit at home and when you walk along the road, when you lie down and when you get up" (Deut 11:19). Though ancient myths reduce humanity to slaves, and modern science reduces humanity to pond scum, the Bible affirms humanity's unique identity as they are intentionally created by God.

Virtually all early civilizations have a creation story. The biblical creation account stands alone in documenting a loving creator who desires to be in connection with His creation. Ancient writings, including those from Egypt, Mesopotamia, and Babylonia, reveal polytheism at the core of their accounts, contrasting the monotheistic biblical creation account. Enuma Elish, the Babylonian creation myth, for example, suggests that the formation of humankind was for the purpose of being in "the service of the gods, and [to] set the gods free."[19] Michael S. Heiser summarizes the words of the Mesopotamian creation myth, noting how it teaches that we were to be slaves for the gods: "He [Marduk] then takes blood from Qingu and mixes it with clay to form humans, who are given the task of digging canals and serving the gods."[20]

Likewise, Leonard W. King describes the Assyrian and Babylonian creation myths as oppressive and submissive, in contrast to the biblical creation account of love and value.[21] The personal relationship with the creator God found in the Genesis account contrasts significantly with the other ancient creation manuscripts. Heiser rightly proposes that the Genesis account's record that God made humankind in His image "elevates humankind above all terrestrial created things so as to exercise benevolent and ethical stewardship over creation."[22] Heiser expounds on the uniqueness of humanity as endorsed by the image of God:

> Every human, regardless of the stage of development, is an imager of God. There is no incremental or partial of the image via some

ability, physical or spiritual. No member of the animal kingdom, regardless of any cognitive ability it might have, is an imager of God. The same goes for any intelligent life form, artificial or the hypothetical extraterrestrial.[23]

Humanity uniquely holds the image of God. This point is further shown as God created humanity on a separate day from the rest of creation, including animals. Humanity alone is to exercise dominion and care of the earth.

The Temptation of Idolatry and Idols

In the Garden, as a result of the Fall, Adam and Eve replaced God with an idol of themselves. Their disobedience unlocked a new ruler for their hearts. Christopher J.H. Wright explains that, as a result of this idolatry, the Lord their God was no longer on the throne of their hearts: "Idolatry begins when we stop listening to God and open our hearts to other gods. At the root, then, all idolatry is human rejection of the Godness of God and the finality of God's moral authority."[24] The Bible repeatedly warns us to guard our hearts—not the physical heart, but the condition of our souls. Once the heart turns to disobedience, all kinds of evil and callousness emerge. Scripture emphasizes "Keep your heart with all diligence, for out of it are the issues of life" (Prov 4:23).

This has implications for addiction, according to Kevin Hoffman, who demonstrates how false attachments are formed when obedience is exchanged for rebellion: "False attachments come because of rebellion against God; they serve as a replacement of the true God with gods—idols, if you will, who fail miserably in comparison to the God who loves humanity and provides for its redemption and reconciliation. Attachment to idols becomes a snare."[25] The exchange of idols for a relationship with God leads to brokenness.

Larry L. Walker and Elmer A. Martens point out how the prophet Isaiah addresses idolatry in the children of Israel: "With ridicule, the prophet describes those who bow down to what they themselves made. The worker makes an idol for himself and then worships this work of his own hands! Modern humans still foolishly worship that which is produced by their own imaginations."[26] Brian Rosner asserts that a renewed relationship through the gospel of Jesus Christ is the solution to sinful, idolatrous behaviors, writing, "In one sense, idolatry is the diagnosis of the human condition to which the gospel is the cure. At root, the problem with humans is not horizontal 'social' problems (like sexual immorality and greed), but rebellion against and replacement of the true and living God with gods that fail (which leads to these destructive sins)."[27] The key to overcoming sin and idolatry is focusing solely on God.

To be fully committed to the Lord, we must choose to eliminate idolatry from our lives. Joshua's direction to the children of Israel is the same to us today:

> Now fear the Lord and serve him with all faithfulness. Throw away the gods your ancestors worshiped beyond the Euphrates River and in Egypt and serve the Lord. But if serving the Lord seems undesirable to you, then choose for yourselves this day whom you will serve, whether the gods your ancestors served beyond the Euphrates, or the gods of the Amorites, in whose land you are living. But as for me and my household, we will serve the Lord (Jos 24:14-15).

History reveals the human story of ongoing idolatrous worship, the battle of the idol of self. Engagement in the conflict against idolatry requires the power of the Holy Spirit, submission to the Word, and repentance.

Michael Ovey offers questions for reflection about our tendency to engage in idolatry. Ovey warns about the echo chamber in which we often speak. There, the words bounce back in our hearing, and we mistake them for the counsel of God. Therefore, when people wrongly believe they have more authority, they create idols of their own making:

> The key question [is] "Who do you worship?" because I can start to analyze what God will look like for someone when I understand who and what they think they are. There is a predictive power in looking at what someone thinks of him or herself for envisaging what his or her god will look like. The two questions "Who do you worship?" and "Who/what do you think you are?" are related.[28]

We must be mindful of setting ourselves and our voice above God. Thinking more of ourselves can lead to idolatrous thought. Ovey suggests that the practice of self-evaluation can reveal the root causes of idols. Such idols, along with other distractions and temptations, will be abandoned when the heart is focused on God.

We need to intentionally eliminate all forms of idolatry. Idols must be completely torn down and replaced with God. Fear, shame, and addiction feed the perversions of the heart, while the remedy found in the Word of God remains unchanging: "You shall love the Lord, your God with all your heart, and with all your soul, and with all your mind" (Matt 22:37). Our relationship with God is maintained through the renewal of our hearts. The Word of God, the catalyst for lasting change, when rightly applied to believers, will keep the heart from vain imaginations.

Trauma and Lies

The spiral of deception hijacks our identity in God. In Romans 1:25, the Apostle Paul reminds readers of what happened to Adam and Eve when "they turned the truth of God into a lie and worshipped and served the creature rather than the Creator, who is blessed forever." The disobedience of the first humans marred their view of the character of God. Allen P. Ross asserts that, in listening to Satan, Adam and Eve no longer saw God as good, loving, and protective: "The tempter also cast doubt over God's character, suggesting that God was jealous, holding them back from their destiny. They would become like God when they ate—and God knew that, according to Satan. So Satan held out to them the promise of divinity—knowing good and evil."[29] The lie took the place of God in their hearts as they sought to prioritize their desires rather than God's.

Tremper Longman rightly portrays the tragic idol of self in the story of Adam and Eve: "Forever God had stamped upon humanity the personal pronoun *mine*, but Adam and Eve tried to erase the divine claim and replace it with their own possessive pronoun, *ours*."[30] Idolatrous hearts replaced the reverent worship of God. Humanity engages in different forms of idolatry, from completely ignoring God to including Him alongside other gods and worshiping them both. Either choice, however, ends in the same sin. As Paul notes, Adam and Eve "served created things rather than the Creator" (Rom 1:25). For the English translation "rather than," according to Stanley Porter, Paul uses the word παρὰ (*para*) in the original text, which denotes the deeper meaning of this verse:

"They worshiped the creature in place of the creator."[31] Ernest Harald Riesenfeld adds that "[παρὰ] does not mean a false worship of God along with a true worship less perfectly fulfilled, but idolatry in place of the worship of God, the Creator being completely ignored."[32] As a result, according to Paul, "they exchanged the truth about God for a lie and worshiped and served created things rather than the Creator—who is forever praised" (Rom 1:25). As Johannes P. Louw and Eugene Albert explain, Paul warns against assigning worth, value, and allegiance to something or someone other than God.[33]

We must fully realize the implications of idol worship in our hearts, which causes us, according to Joseph Henry Thayer, to "omit or pass by the Creator."[34] William Sanday and Arthur C. Headlam maintain that the preposition, παρὰ, signifies, "not merely 'more than the Creator' but passing by the Creator altogether … to the neglect of the Creator" becomes the thread that weaves throughout humanity as we ignore God for a lifeless idol of our own creation.[35]

Deceptive beliefs common to humankind include the following: 1) that humanity does not need God, which challenges authority; 2) that humankind is not unique, which challenges the image of God; and 3) that humankind is not valuable, which challenges dignity. We must exchange our perspectives on God, replacing disobedience with obedience, independence with dependence, and unbelief with trust. The serpent sows doubt about God's character, leading to disobedience. The qualities of God, along with His love and intentions for humankind, have been distorted through lies. Satan plants these lies in our hearts, which manifest through the body, with the intention of corrupting the image of God in humanity.

All lies involve bearing false witness against God or others. The Lord hates false witness, as seen in Deuteronomy, where it states, "You shall not bear false witness against your neighbor" (Deut 5:20). Throughout biblical history, lies have often been believed, leading to serious consequences. Rebellion, distraction, disobedience, and an unfulfilled future are some of the results of partnering with lies. Ultimately, Jesus Christ reverses the enemy's lies and satisfies the requirements of sacrifice, removing the veil and restoring the relationship between humanity and God.

Creative Encounters with God

Art Is the Language

Some regard art as an offense to the church, claiming that the visual arts distract from worship of God. However, Scripture demonstrates that the Lord utilized the arts in designing the Temple, specifying colors and details to create splendor (Exod 25-27; 1 Kgs 6-7). God is the Master Artist and the creative arts flow from Him (Ps 19:1; Exod 35:31–32, 35)! Deborah Sokolove points out how art mediates between the mundane and the divine. She explains how art is both therapeutic and transformative: "As a spiritual practice, making art is valued primarily for the subjective experience of the maker in the process of making, and often practitioners see more truth in the faltering handstamp of the earnest beginner than in the practiced ease of the well-trained."[36] Beyond the finished product is the process of artmaking. Often, the process is where healing comes. As one meditates on God with a few simple art supplies, a creative opportunity is opened in the heart. Creative expression offers healthy ways to come nearer to God, according to Gary Thomas: "One of the most powerful antidotes to addiction is participating in different activities that lift addicts out of themselves and into positive, constructive acts of creation."[37]

Art is a transformative communication tool. Ted Harrison, a broadcast journalist and television producer, became an artist at the age of sixty, after realizing the limitations of language to express ideas:

> Language is what we use to form, shape and then express our ideas, to issue instructions, or to share news, but there come moments when we are lost for words. And not just at times of shock or wonder, but in everyday situations. Try describing a pain to a doctor or a lovely smell to a friend. … It's impossible to convey what you are truly experiencing. … When it comes to describing religious experiences, language is especially inadequate. … It's through art forms that … the greater ideas can be expressed and conveyed. Music, painting, sculpture, and dance, for instance, can approach the Transcendent without being weighted down by words and arguments over their exact meanings.[38]

In creativity, words are unnecessary. Art is the language.

The merits of art are numerous and often overlooked by present-day society, according to Swiss theologian and pastor Beat Rink, who founded Crescendo International to bring the creative arts to churches around the world. Rink, exploring how art affects people, the church, and the community, lists four outcomes of art: "Art satisfies the thirst for beauty; art is of service in *delectare*, i.e., joy and relaxation; the enjoyment of art as a process of purification and liberation; and art as a means of solving problems and as a place to seek truth."[39] Rink points out that creativity flows from God, and it serves us as a "way out of an unhealthy attitude to life" through the "cooperation of one's own will" with what God is doing in one's life. This, he says, "brings the desired fruit" in one's life.[40]

Restoration through Creativity

An opportunity exists to promote ongoing spiritual growth for those recovering from life-controlling addictions. Christian addicts are part of church communities and require targeted support. Restoration is achievable through learning and applying Scripture, experiencing spiritual encounters with God, and participating in a healthy community. This book addresses individuals battling addiction and the leaders who support the deeper spiritual needs of the recovery community in the church. Our churches are made up of people who absorb information in different ways, including auditory means, such as stories; tactile means, such as kinesthetic experiences; visual means, such as artistic endeavors; as well as reading and writing.

Different learning styles require different presentations for effective information absorption. According to Jessa Hernandez et al., "Visual learners prefer depictions of information as figures and charts. Auditory learners prefer to hear the information as lectures and discussions. Read/write learners prefer information presented as text based. Kinesthetic learners prefer concrete experiences that connect the material to reality."[41] According to VARK Learn Ltd., to impact kinesthetic learners, "ideas need to be practical and relevant to you, and you need to do things to understand them."[42] The store shelves and resource libraries are filled with devotions and written materials that focus on learning styles centered on reading and writing. However, there are few resources available for kinesthetic learners. Kinesthetic learners can explore and embrace Scripture through fun, creative methods that make learning both engaging and meaningful.

Exercising creativity through art projects may be uncomfortable for many; however, research reveals that some discomfort is necessary for character growth.

In discussing spiritual formation, Griffin Gooch suggests that "set regimens of discipline might best be supplemented by the addition of preternatural practices, going outside of our preferred norms, and engaging with God in ways that do not directly match our comfortable ideals."[43] In other words, it is beneficial to engage in a different kind of spiritual discipline, such as encountering God through creative expression.

Each chapter in this book ends with a creative prompt that will help you connect your story to the character. This method of learning might trigger anxiety for some of you, while for others, creativity will come easily. Either way, I am excited to facilitate a connection to God through creativity and to share this experience as your creative story unfolds! For those who are unsure of creative expression, and to those who easily express through imagination, you are safe, free from judgment, courageous, and bold. You're not alone as you embark on this adventure! The Holy Spirit is with you and will guide you into all truth. Creative encounters specifically make space for the Holy Spirit to move and reveal God. Remember, He desires to interact with us, and creativity is a beautiful way to do so.

Keep the following tips in mind as you work through each creative exercise throughout the book:

- Focus on connecting your heart to God. It does not

matter what your creative skill level is or how you would rate your art for beauty or worth.

- If you are in a group setting, imagine that you are in a bubble with the Holy Spirit, isolated from all other influences. Creativity with God brings new opportunities for interacting with Him. As we remove distractions, we make room for the Holy Spirit to work.

- Avoid commenting on your own work or other's work as this tends to shift the focus away from intimacy with God.

- Avoid making the focus of your canvas about an old belief or mindset. Instead, focus on showing the creative healing portion of your story.

- Cover the canvas with color and/or images. Avoid leaving white space.

A suggested list of supplies to gather includes canvas, magazines (local libraries offer free magazines), old picture books, abandoned hymnals, unloved Bibles, sponge applicator, markers, scissors, various paints, glue, Mod Podge, random ephemera, and heavyweight paper. For pyrography, you will need to have a wood burner, planks of raw wood, or a new plain cutting board. With the recent rise in awareness of creativity, many stores now carry art supplies. Supplies are easily found at discount, hobby, and chain stores (e.g., Dollar Store, Walmart, Michaels, Hobby Lobby).

Use the chapter prompt or make up your own artistic exercise to explore during this time with God. Glue, paint, draw, and canvas the response to the question and impression you are receiving from God. Use all your supplies or a selection of them. Feel free to alter with paint, rip, or distress. When using Mod Podge, be sure to add enough so that the paper is completely adhered to the canvas; otherwise, it will lift and bubble. Don't worry, it will dry clear.

Before starting each creative session, pray aloud the following prayer (or one of your own), inviting the Lord to join you:

Holy Spirit, guide me as I encounter truth today. I invite you to speak to my heart through my imagination and creativity. You are here, and I am safe. I activate my mind, will, and emotions, placing myself in a space to create, express, and understand Biblical truth. I want to genuinely experience and encounter You. Thank you for revealing the truth, as I align with the Word of God. In the powerful name of Jesus. Amen.

CHAPTER 2: IMAGE OF JOURNEY

Introduction

Biblical characters and their life stories illustrate how imagery is applicable for spiritual development. Michael Humphries agrees on the importance of imagery in Scripture and its role in conveying meaning: "Images abound in the biblical literature; and certainly the study of images, including the close reading of metaphors and similes, elicits a better understanding of the various themes and perceptions of the world contained in the specific writings of the Hebrew and Christian Scriptures."[44] Furthermore, imagery serves as a connection point for memory and recall. The use of images in biblical writing demonstrates that the stories and lessons shared are memorable. The Bible conveys its truths through illustrations, typology, imagery, symbolism, and parables. Even Jesus regularly used imagery as He conveyed His message through impactful parables.[45]

Genesis 12 reveals an image of a journey that starts when Abram leaves his homeland. God established a fundamental principle that His people must separate themselves from any hindrance to fulfilling His purpose for their lives. The journey of obedience continues as Abraham travels through the land in obedience and faith. He receives a covenant from God, which includes protection, reward, descendants, and the Promised Land (Gen 15).

Abraham

Genesis 12 introduces the imagery of the journey in the narrative of the call of Abram: "The Lord had said to Abram, 'Leave your country, your people, and your father's household and go to the land I will show you'" (v.1).[46] The Hebrew verb for walking is *hālak*. Allen Myers notes that this verb is also used in the Mishnah as "a teaching or precept that serves as a practical guide for living … to indicate how one lives out the commandments … in its basic sense, a teaching or precept that serves as a practical guide for living; also spelled Halachah, Halakah."[47] David Rosenberg notes that *halakah* can refer to "a specific teaching on a point of

Jewish law."[48] Additionally, Rabbi Meir promotes the use of *halacha, aggadah* (narratives), and *meshalim* (parables) to train students in Torah. Utilizing three-part wisdom, Meir effectively schools Jewish children for successful living: "It's Jewish law that guides everyday life. From prayer to business deals, from Shabbos (Sabbath) rules to how we treat others, halacha shows us the path. The Hebrew word itself means 'to walk'—because these laws are the path Jews walk through life."[49]

Jewish people later established *halakhah* for their daily lives, according to Mike and Sue Dowgiewicz. Derived from *hālak*, they explain, "a halakhah is the way God's work was interpreted and applied consistently to a particular situation. The emphasis was not on interpretation alone but on correct application, hence the walking part."[50] Some examples of intentional actions expressing one's beliefs could include the following: I believe God can be known; therefore, I extend energy and attention to cultivate my relationship with Him; I believe that family is a gift to be treasured; therefore, I am attentively investing in the next generation; or I believe I am a minister of reconciliation; therefore, I seek opportunities to share the redemptive story with others.

I suggest that the practice of creating rules for living would benefit modern households. Jewish families engaged in daily practices to express what Scripture taught. Perhaps the recovery community could intentionally address distractive behavior by reintroducing this practice into their lives. Healthy habits are another form of rules for living. Creating a discipline of actionable habits can enhance daily recovery efforts.

The concept of journey appears throughout Scripture, both figuratively and literally. God revealed to Abraham throughout the journey that He is a personal God. In addition to obedience, the virtue of faith is evident in the study of Abraham's biblical character. The Lord establishes His name with Abraham and prepares a people for himself. Christopher J. H. Wright celebrates the one true God who desires a relationship with humankind:

> YHWH presents himself as the God who wills to be known. This self-communicating drive is involved in everything God does in creation, revelation, salvation, and judgment. Human beings therefore are summoned to know YHWH as God on the clear assumption that they can know him and that God wills that they should know him.[51]

This discovery leads Abraham to forsake all other gods in

favor of the one true God, Yahweh.

Ronald Clements emphasizes that Scripture reveals God as relatable and personal, unlike the pagan gods. While the gods of Mesopotamia were worshipped and feared, the God of Scripture "speaks to man, gives him commandments, makes promises, foretells the destiny of his descendants, etc." [52]God builds intimacy, and Abraham receives an inheritance as he remains faithful to Him. God wanted people to understand His true nature, and by establishing a covenant with Abraham, He corrected the misconceptions humanity had created. The awe and reverence of the Lord are evident in Abraham's interaction, as he does not withhold Isaac as a sacrifice (22:12). False gods and their images were being dethroned as the loving, personal God was being revealed.

While examining Abraham as an image of a journey, we observe that he abandoned the idols and gods of his people. Notice that Abraham came from a pagan culture that did not worship Yahweh. Idolatry is the worship of false gods or reliance upon anything or anyone other than the one true God. The ancient idols represented the gods of one's ancestors, community, or local deities. These deities were thought to bestow good fortune on those who honored them. John H. Walton further explains how the ancient people viewed gods: "The gods were connected to the forces of nature and showed themselves through natural phenomena. ... [They] did not reveal their natures or give any idea of what would bring their favor or wrath. ... [They] were worshipped by being flattered, cajoled, humored, and appeased. Manipulation is the operative term."[53] F.B. Huey indicates that the patriarchs acknowledged the existence of other gods by recounting how their ancestors served pagan deities. As Huey rightly points out, the patriarchs ultimately worshiped the one true God: "Abraham probably worshiped the Mesopotamian moon god Sin before God made a covenant with him," yet as the patriarchs "became worshipers of the only living God, their descendants reverted to polytheism, worshiping the many gods of the Canaanite fertility cults (Exod 32; Num 25:1–3; Josh 24:14; Ezek 6:13; 20:8). The prophets constantly condemned the people for their worship of their neighbors' gods."[54] Scripture is filled with warnings and rebukes against turning to foreign gods. It has been (and still is) a continuous battle for the people of God.

Joshua 24 highlights the polytheistic culture of the era, stating, "This is what the Lord, the God of Israel, says: 'Long ago, your forefathers, including Terah, the father of Abraham and Nahor, lived beyond the River, and worshiped other gods." Verse 14 continues with the well-known call for a decision:

Now fear the Lord and serve Him with all faithfulness. Throw away the gods your forefathers worshiped beyond the River and in Egypt and serve the Lord. But if serving the Lord seems undesirable to you, then choose for yourselves this day whom you will serve, whether the gods your forefathers served beyond the River, or the gods of the Amorites, in whose land you are living. But as for me and my household, we will serve the Lord (Joshua 24:14).

Abraham abandoned his community's deities and left his family security, inheritance, and safety in pursuit of an unknown god. Abraham chose to pursue the promises of God. A spiritual journey involves forsaking oneself for a wholehearted pursuit of God. Abraham demonstrated this connection by abandoning everything in exchange for the promise of something greater. Paul taught that, to obtain Christ, one must be emptied of all other aspirations (1 Cor 7:29–32).

Abraham's connection with God began as he responded to YHWH's call and their relationship was solidified through obedience. YHWH initiated this relationship with a personal invitation. The notion of an interpersonal relationship with a deity was unprecedented; ancient idols were unapproachable and lacked personal interaction. Abraham marked the encounters that he had with God with pillars and altars for future generations. John Beck asserts that these commemorations; "building altars, establishing tombs, erecting pillars, and digging wells were how Abraham's family also connected to the land."[55] Walton offers a different perspective, arguing that they were a means of establishing Israel: "Altars function as sacrificial platforms, and their construction can also mark the introduction of the worship of a particular god in a new land."[56] These altars marked the beginning of places of worship for future generations. The Lord appeared to Abram at Shechem, at the oak of Moreh, a site of worship, and Abram built an altar to the Lord, who had appeared to him (Gen 12:7). Continuing to Bethel, he built another altar to the Lord and called on His name. Upon returning from Negev to Bethel, he called on the name of the Lord at the site where he had first erected an altar (13:4). Settling by the oaks of Mamre in Hebron, he built yet another altar to the Lord there (13:18).

Abraham interacted with the land in ways that may seem unfamiliar to contemporary Western culture. James Hastings described the first deeded land as the Machpelah cave, designated as Sarah's burial site. Purchased from the Hittites, this ownership granted Abraham an irrevocable right to the property. Hastings explains, "Here Sarah was buried by her husband; and subsequently Abraham himself, Isaac, Rebekah, Leah, and Jacob were laid to rest in the same spot (Gen 49:31)."[57] They did not own land, plant crops, or settle. In the midst of Abraham's great loss, the Promised Land was being established.

Abraham left his lifestyle and his family and obediently followed the word from God: "Go to a land I will show you" (Gen 12:1). Walton reminds us of the significance of Abraham's sacrifices: "When Abram gave up his place in his father's household, he forfeited his security. He was putting his survival, identity, future, and his security in the Lord's hands."[58] Furthermore, Abraham followed the Lord's command when he sought to sacrifice his only son, an act that would have voided his hope and the promise of the heir. Abraham wrestled with whether God was good and faithful to his promises. Would Abraham instead choose to have his son live and accept the temporary blessing that came with the heir? Abraham had to trust in the covenant God made with him. This discipline of obedience is a significant theme in Abraham's life as his faith deepens with each encounter with the Lord.

This promise to protect Abraham can be observed after the battle to rescue Lot, his possessions, and the people, where God proclaims in Genesis 15:1, "Do not fear, Abram. I am your shield, your exceedingly great reward." God promises to continue protecting and supporting Abram. His journey involves fostering faith in God: "Abram believed the Lord, and He credited it to him as righteousness" (Gen 15:6). Abram's faith and belief reflect his devotion and submission to God's plans.

The covenant to Abram, as found in Scripture, is this: "I will be their God" (Gen 17:8). God makes this great promise to lead, guide, and promote Israel. The journey of obedience intensifies as God commands Abraham to sacrifice Isaac, the promised son, on an altar. The first revelation that the Lord will provide is revealed as Abraham proceeds to sacrifice his heir. Along the journey, Abram is renamed Abraham and encounters El Shaddai, the Almighty God to whom nothing is impossible. God is a shield and a great reward.

Abraham, the patriarch of Israel, Clements explains, was also known as "the ancestor of all Israel, … a military leader, … a priestly intercessor for his people, … a prophet, … and an example of human piety and human obedience to God."[59] The patriarch receives the promise from God for a grand mission, according to Wright: "The call of Abraham included the promise that through his descendants God intended to bring blessing to all the nations of the earth. … Ultimately, Israel existed for the sake of the nations."[60] The image of obedience brought the blessing of God and the birth of His nation.

Spiritual formation is meant to change us into the likeness of God, according to Evan Howard. The journey Abraham took was a pilgrimage through which obedience led to transformation: "Pilgrimage—a journey from the starting place to a holy destination, a journey wherein the person who finishes the journey is different than the person who began it. During a pilgrimage, one encounters catalysts, forces that stimulate change."[61] Abraham's journey remains transformative throughout his story. Although Abraham never saw the Promised Land, he had faith that his descendants would see it.

Journey of Obedience

Obedience not only affects your relationship with God, according to Gary Hardin, but it also affects your relationship with others: "Obedience [means] to hear God's Word and act accordingly."[62] As we journey with God in obedient behavior, our actions affect those around us in positive ways that glorify God. If we think that our lives are ineffective to others, we are deceived. Your sobriety is about you but not all about you. God desires to bring a blessing to others through your obedient life.

How is God guiding you on this journey of obedience? Maybe you have a mentor, a spouse, a friend, a rehabilitation program, a church family, or an influential book. Reflect on how God is guiding your steps toward Him. Reflect on the things, people, and familiar places left behind to pursue sober living and God's calling.

Wendy Buttacy exposes the nature of addiction while clearly defining idols. Addiction is known to overwhelm a person. The choices, cravings, and desires seem uncontrollable. Buttacy writes, "An idol is anything we set up as a god in our lives; we worship it and bow down to it. We let it dictate what we do. Our desire for these idols take center stage instead of God's will for our lives."[63] Wright reminds us that God desires to have the only place in our hearts, not a place shared with others. God intends to be glorified by all of His creation. This is a significant reason why addiction is so powerful: it vies for the place that belongs only to God. Wright then elaborates on the topic by providing a simple list of idols, which include "things we fear, things we trust, and things we need."[64] This breakdown is a modest yet effective list to identify idols in our lives. Kyle Idleman offers a symptom checker of the heart to identify areas of concern. His list includes "What worries you? What do you complain about? What disappoints you? Where do you make a financial sacrifice? What infuriates you? Where's your sanctuary?"[65]

Idols change over time, from Elvis to Jelly Roll. Examples of cultural idols that may keep us from God include the obvious, such as substance addiction. However, not all idols are illegal. Gambling, marijuana, and alcohol are legal in most states. Other idols seem rather innocent: overspending, grandchildren or children, gossip, goals, and work, among others. Idolatry is prevalent in much of our culture; the question is: What or whom are you serving and sacrificing to? We all bow to something.

The addiction recovery community must actively participate in introspection and spiritual discipleship. I love the Teen Challenge model of self-evaluation. It includes questions that concern a behavior, an attitude, or a choice made by the student.[66] The student then contemplates a series of questions that consider the results of their action, its impact on their relationship with Christ, and its effect on others. This worksheet is crucial for taking ownership of one's actions and making necessary, healthy changes. Following God requires a radical move in the opposite direction from one's previous trajectory.

Creative Encounter

Let's imagine your journey. An image is a powerful expression of where you have been and where you are heading. What things have you left behind? What idols did you abandon? Find images that illustrate your journey of obedience and sobriety. Using a map, compass, or trail as the basc image, create a collage of your sobriety adventure. Perhaps an image of you moving forward, away from disobedience.

Make sure to incorporate the hindrances that would keep you from receiving your promised land. Remember to insert the truth, which is larger than the sin/hindrances. Is there something you are clutching that God wants you to release? Conduct a self-evaluation by examining your current attitudes, desires, and habits. Add this to your canvas as a declaration of obedient compliance toward God.

Application

What if our obedience releases the blessing of God upon us? Do you wonder if Abraham ever asked God, "Are we there yet?" I think our journey is longer than we imagined. Sobriety and health is an ongoing journey toward God, and our final destination is heaven. How has God guided this journey of obedience? Reflect on the things, people, and familiar places left behind to pursue sober living and follow God's calling. Like Abraham's journey, you may leave behind generational idols. Do not be intimidated that you are the only person in your family to serve and obey God. He will strengthen you as He did Abraham.

Idols cannot be a part of the solution for your new life. Do not edit your idolatrous heart—get a complete transplant. Gregory Beale has an effective way of looking at idolatry that includes a reminder that humanity was created to reflect the Creator. If we are revering God, we will resemble Him. If we idolize the world, we will become a reflection of it. Beale states simply, "What people revere, they resemble, either for ruin or restoration."[67] This has me examining myself in a mirror.

Thick patches often cover the road. Weeds and branches block the way, and ruts from past choices seem to pull you back to that old trail. Be courageous, friend. God is calling us to a new life—a life of destiny, promise, and future. A life of reflecting His glory.

CHAPTER 3: IMAGE OF STRUGGLE

Introduction

Jacob's story reveals his struggles with deception and forgiveness for many issues in his life. He needed forgiveness for taking advantage of Esau and for deceptive behavior toward Isaac. He also had to learn to forgive his father-in-law for his deception against him, and, later, Jacob struggles with God as he prepares to reconcile with his brother Esau after deceiving him twenty years earlier. Jacob embodies the imagery of struggle. Despite his backstory as a deceiver and living in a culture overwhelmed by paganism and idol worship, however, he managed to grow and flourish.

Don Allen Tennison rightly views struggle as a form of growth, stating, "Spiritual formation may be defined as a struggle because of the intentionality involved in the change from one person to another person."[68] He notes that God used a life of struggles to form Jacob in remarkable ways: "Jacob goes on a journey not unlike Abraham, but he is named Israel for his struggle with God and man."[69] Gary D. Baldwin's portrayal of the patriarch includes the Hebrew meaning for Jacob: "He grasps the heel. … He cheats, supplants."[70] Baldwin emphasizes struggles as a part of Jacob's existence when he writes, "Jacob's story is a story of conflict. The note of conflict is even heard before his birth (Gen 25:22–23). However, in the midst of the all-too-human quarrels over family and fortune, God was at work protecting and prospering His blessed."[71] The *Merriam-Webster Dictionary* defines "struggle" as making "strenuous or forceful efforts in the face of difficulties or opposition; to proceed with difficulty or with great effort."[72]

Jacob's behavior mirrored that of his parents, Isaac and

Rebekah. Isaac deceived King Abimelech when he, out of fear, lied about the identity of his beautiful wife (Gen 26:7). Rebekah and her brother Laban both had deceptive tendencies. Genesis 27 describes how Rebekah encouraged her son to deceive Isaac for the blessing of the firstborn. She also provided the clothing and food for Jacob to use in tricking his father (vv. 15-16). Later, the family's trait of deception reappears in the wedding bed fiasco (29:21-26), when Laban deceives his nephew Jacob by swapping in the eldest daughter for the beloved Rachel as Jacob's new bride (v. 23). The heritage of deception can also be seen in Abraham, Jacob's grandfather, who twice concealed his marriage to the beautiful Sarah (12:10-20; 20:1-18).

Jacob

Jacob's story includes formative encounters, including his personal encounter with the Lord at Bethel, which inspires him to commit to giving a tenth of all that God gives him, along with his declaration that the Lord will be his God (Gen 28:20-22): "Then Jacob made a vow, saying, 'If God will be with me and will watch over me on this journey I am taking and will give me food to eat and clothes to wear so that I return safely to my father's household, then the Lord will be my God and this stone that I have set up as a pillar will be God's house, and of all that you give me I will give you a tenth.'" God reveals himself to Jacob, promising land, protection, and offspring (vv. 13–15). On his journey to find a wife, he is greatly encouraged by the Lord.

Jacob also struggled to reconcile with his brother Esau. Jacob had deceived Esau twenty years earlier and feared meeting him. After dividing his family and flocks, he wrestles with God one night at the place he named Peniel (Gen 32:24–30). John Skinner observes that, although there is no repentance, Jacob offers a standard prayer for assistance: "Jacob's prayer, consisting of an invocation, thanksgiving, petition, and appeal to the divine faithfulness, is a classic model of OT devotion though the element of confession, so prominent in later supplications, is significantly absent."[73] Craig Keener adds valuable insight on the wrestling encounter, stating that it lends the origin for Jacob's name change and "marks the Jacob/Israel shift from an outcast and usurper to the heir of the covenant and the chosen leader of God's people."[74]

Part of the struggle that Jacob underwent included submission to God. Watchman Nee reminds believers of their weaknesses through the story of Jacob: "When we begin to look at Jacob the man, we discover how strikingly his story is like our own. Before God has begun to deal with us, we are inclined to take a rather superior attitude to Jacob and judge him as self-willed and irresponsible."[75] God has His way in the wrestle, and Nee asserts that this struggle "illustrates God's method of dealing with us. It is finally weakening us so that we cannot rise. God has His way of doing this with each of us. Jacob was stronger than most, but God conquered."[76]

Since the time he was in the womb, Jacob's name has remained synonymous with struggle. He faced many struggles throughout his life. He struggled to promote himself and claimed Esau's birthright through the exchange of a bowl of lentil stew (Gen 25:29-34). Through deception, Jacob received the blessing of the firstborn (27:27). Additionally, he faced trickery from Laban regarding marriage to Rachel. The struggle with Laban mirrored Jacob's deception with Esau, but God used Laban to discipline Jacob, refining and proving his character (29:16-30). Jacob's life story, which is marked by lies and deception, reveals that God brings change through struggles. Formation into the person God desires is a positive work of struggle as we pursue God's blessing and plans.

Struggle For Change

The positive effects of struggle are not always obvious. Many struggles originate from childhood trauma and influences. As we grow, we often find that our experiences don't align with our perspectives. Conflicts can arise when negative childhood experiences clash with current situations. When positive growth occurs, we might reject love or struggle to accept approval if we were raised in an emotionally negative environment. Mindsets develop early in childhood and influence how we respond to challenges.

We can identify certain mindsets and thought patterns that do not align with Scripture and adjust them to match God's Word. Those mindsets that no longer serve us can be replaced with new, healthy thoughts. Caroline Leaf researches the connection between mind-body health and productive thinking. Her work in epigenetics, the study of how one's environment, behaviors, and lifestyle can change the way genes function without altering the DNA, is at the forefront of mind science.[77] She advocates harnessing the mind's power to cultivate healthy thoughts and habits:

> A mindset is an attitude or a cluster of thoughts with attached information and emotions that generate a particular perception. They shape how you see and interact with the world. They can catapult you forward, allowing you to achieve your dreams, or put you in reverse drive if you are not careful. A mindset is therefore a significant mental resource and source of power.

> Your mindsets set your expectation levels, which
> will either be positive or negative.[78]

Our thought life manifests in our physical bodies, for our benefit or our demise. Hopelessness, unforgiveness, and ingratitude all have negative outcomes for our health.

Hopelessness can be reversed through gratitude and by focusing on positive truths such as those found in Scripture. Daniel Amen discusses the impact of long-term negative thinking. He points to studies suggesting that those with Alzheimer's have harmful toxins built up in the brain. He notes, "Negative thoughts cause your brain to immediately release chemicals that affect every cell in your body, making you feel bad; while the opposite is also true—positive, happy, hopeful thoughts release chemicals that make you feel good."[79] The brain imaging done at his clinic provides insight into brain health and sheds light on brain disorders. This information can motivate change in habits and thoughts.

Ingratitude breeds pride, self-righteousness, and despair. Jesus gives us the answer for ingratitude when He directs us to love one another. One of the main characteristics of gratitude is its other-focused nature. Charlie Self et al. also speak passionately about gratitude and its effects: "Gratitude also arises from a sense of awe and wonder as we ponder the character and nature of our Lord and the magnificence of His creation."[80] Forming our attitudes and mindset based on Scripture is an essential step toward a healthy spirit, mind, and body. A positive connection with God during life's struggles offers encouragement to keep growing and moving toward complete victory. Daniel Amen coined the term ANTS, automatic negative thoughts, "to describe how negativity can infest your brain."[81] This infestation can be turned around by using Amen's techniques to reprogram one's thought life. Comprehensive studies have been conducted by top scientists on thinking, physical health, and optimal brain function. The good news is that we can change our brains. We can direct new thoughts to bring positive emotions and health.

People relate and connect to God in different ways, according to Gary Thomas. He identifies nine different ways that people can encounter God, calling them spiritual temperaments or pathways: "Naturalist: let me be outdoors. Sensate: let me experience. Traditionalist: let me remember. Ascetic: let me be alone. Activist: let me conquer. Caregiver: let me care. Enthusiast: let me celebrate. Contemplative: let me feel. Intellectual: let me think."[82]

The art encounters in this resource especially resonate with the sensate temperaments. Thomas cites medical research that underscores the role of sight and images in affecting our decisions, our wellbeing, and our faith: "As much as a third of our cerebral cortex, which is the highest level of our brain, is devoted to visual processing. Researchers have even found that sight can be used to affect our will, which has a direct bearing on our commitment to live out our faith."[83] If you are a sensate, one who relishes life and worship through the five senses, you may especially appreciate the creative encounter using the image of struggle.

Our thinking and ruminations create mindsets, a framework for thoughts. When we take control of our thinking, our mindsets will change. As we consider His omnipotence, majesty, and love for humanity, affirming thoughts will flood our minds. One way to explore new ideas is through setting aside time for thinking. Caroline Leaf encourages this daily practice for brain health and clarity. Our culture is often fast-paced, which leaves little time to think deeply. Leaf's research shows that quieting oneself with uninterrupted meditation and free time to ponder is valuable for brain health. She extolls the benefits of exploring all of one's senses during this thinking time: "When we choose to truly tune in to the now—to see, listen, feel, move, taste, and inhale the present, using all our senses to soak up the minute beauty of the moment—we enhance our thinking and thereby enhance our ability to learn and succeed at life."[84] Using thinking time to engage our imagination and visually connect with our struggle brings about the transformation from the wrestle. Thinking time is a useful tool for spiritual growth.

Creative Encounter

What image comes to your mind when you consider struggle? What issue or attitude have you wrestled with? What will be gained at the end of the wrestling match? Imagine the positive result and outcome on the other side of the struggle. You may be wrestling with forgiving yourself or others for the past, stepping into a new identity, or releasing old mindsets. Either way, God is guiding you toward healthy spiritual formation through struggles and wrestling.

Using the questions above, create a representation of the promise or other side of the struggle. What does the payoff for wrestling look like to you? For instance, although staying clean is a struggle, the payoff is that my children are with me. Select images from magazines, books, or pictures that represent the promise you're fighting for. Use Mod Podge to create a collage. Imagine the other side of struggle, relational wholeness, renewed identity, and a hope-filled life.

Application

We often struggle with various issues, including mindsets, identity, false beliefs, and lies that we have believed about God, ourselves, or others. Shelly Hogan launches attacks on ungodly mindsets in her teaching and preaching sessions, warning that "entrenched thought patterns, besetting sins, and inflicted wounds all conspire to entrap humanity and hinder true freedom offered by Christ in salvation. The enemy of our soul works to ensnare through the weaponries of offense, lies, and temptations."[85] Hogan maintains that healing is possible for the followers of Jesus through repentance and forgiveness. Recovering truth in all areas of our lives is paramount to successful sobriety. We must acknowledge mindsets that no longer serve us and, instead, allow the Spirit to renew our minds.

In God's creation, struggles in nature can signify resilience and strength as well, such as the adult butterfly wriggling free from its chrysalis.[86] Other examples include the chick fighting to break out of the egg. The chick embryo grows by consuming the nutrients in the egg sac until it's time to hatch and struggles to break free from the shell. It has a small egg tooth on its beak to help peel the shell. The chick uses the remaining nutrients in the eggshell to fight and struggle to break free of the shell. Likewise, struggles are seen with salmon, which swim upstream from the ocean waters to find a place to lay eggs. According to National Geographic, "Salmon are known for their grueling migrations. All species are born in freshwater streams and migrate to the ocean as juveniles. Sockeye salmon stay for up to three years in their natal habitat—longer than any other salmon. … Ten to 40 percent of female Atlantic salmon, however, survive and return to the sea."[87] We don't struggle in the same way as salmon, dodging rapids, bears, and eagles looking for food!

Chances are, however, that your current struggle is forming you. Maybe God designed the situation to cause you to grow and mature, like the butterfly, the chick, or the salmon. The strong and resilient will endure. Struggle transforms us as we dig for truth, refuse to submit to our flesh, and, instead, turn upstream toward God.

CHAPTER 4: IMAGE OF ASCENT

Introduction

Ascending means going upward, as in drawing closer to God. We must move toward God while intentionally seeking His will. Isaiah Hoogendyk describes ascent as "an upward slope, as in a mountain or path."[88] Moments of encounter on mountaintops serve as a testament to others, reflecting God's glory to those around us. Moses exemplifies the idea of ascent as he rises to meet the Lord and then shares the experience with God's people. There, in the presence of God, Moses seeks forgiveness for the sins of the Israelites, and God reveals His forgiving nature. Like Moses, we must pursue God intentionally, ascending to meet the Lord and seek forgiveness.

Moses

The image of ascent, according to Don Allen Tennison, represents spiritual formation in the life of Moses: "Like Abraham, Jacob, and Joseph, Moses journeyed, struggled, led, and remained faithful to God throughout it, but Moses also ascended to God. ... Spiritual formation as an ascent [is] understood as a drawing nearer to God."[89] The ascent of Moses's spiritual formation began in the home of his birth family, during a time when Pharaoh had ordered the deaths of every Hebrew baby boy (Exod 1:22). Moses's mother, Jochabed, sought to save Moses by placing him in a waterproof basket among the reeds of the bank of the Nile, where Pharaoh's daughter discovered him, defied Pharaoh's order, and made him her son (2:1-10). Eugene Carpenter notes that Moses's story illustrates the sovereignty of God: "God's actions and words display his wisdom, ingenuity, power, and ability to thwart all plans made to abolish his people. Yahweh will use all the forces of education and wisdom that the Egyptians can offer to train his chosen leader in the very palace of the king and his people."[90] It is reassuring to know that God will influence both people and hearts as He advances His plan for humanity. God used the oppressive Egyptians, the cry of a newborn baby, and the kindness of the Pharaoh's daughter to advance God's mission.

Through God's plan for humanity, Moses rose to a position of prominence in Pharaoh's palace, where he benefitted from the advantages of royalty and wealth, receiving training in rhetoric, art, diplomatic leadership, and instruction in foreign languages from royal tutors.[91] Dewayne Bryan also notes, however, that the Egyptian culture that Moses grew up in was deeply rooted in pagan worship of "a vast number of gods, nearly 1,500 of which were known by name."[92] Despite the widespread idolatry around him, Moses formed a relationship with the one true God.

After Moses flees to Midian and marries Zipporah, he has the first transformative encounter at Horeb, the mountain of God, while "tending the flock of Jethro his father-in-law, the priest of Midian" (Exod 3:1). As he passes a bush that burned without being consumed, he hears the Lord's voice from within it. He commemorates that divine moment by taking off his shoes while standing on holy ground (v. 5).

The encounter, a theophany, are not usually described in detail but, rather, are described as awe-inspiring and fear-inspiring. According to Cecil P. Straton they can come in a variety of forms: "Earthquake, thunder, lightning, storm wind, shofar blasts, brightness, and darkness suggest God's nearness" (Exod 19:16, 18–19).[93]

According to Scripture, the burning bush represents an encounter with the Holy God who revealed himself to Moses as "I AM WHO I AM" (Exod 3:14). Other recorded theophanies include a cloud by day and a pillar of fire at night, and God appearing to individuals such as Hagar, Elijah, and Abraham.[94] Theodore Hiebert notes that theophanies most often occur on mountains because "the mountain was considered that point in the environment most conducive to contact with the divine, most revelatory of divine presence."[95] Walton agrees, adding that "in the ancient and classical world, deities were normally believed to have their dwelling places on mountains."[96]

The Bible records several theophanies that occurred outside mountain settings. They are described as occurring under an oak tree (Judg 6:11-24), in the temple (Isa 6:1-13), and by a river (Ezek 1:1-3:15). Another image of ascent reveals Moses's identity as an intercessor who seeks God's forgiveness for the sins of the Israelites. Moses as intercessor must be seen within the context of the giving of the Mosaic

Law at Mount Sinai. God establishes a covenant with His people and gives the laws for their blessing and purity, as well as the design for the tabernacle.

The Law includes moral, civil, and ceremonial requirements. Exodus chronicles the intercession for the people of God during this ascent to the mountain, when Moses receives the Law: "So Moses went back to the Lord and said, 'Oh, what a great sin these people have committed! They have made themselves gods of gold. But now, please forgive their sin— but if not, then blot me out of the book you have written" (32:31-32). Warren Wiersbe points out that God twice threatens to "destroy Israel and use Moses to find a new nation, but [Moses] refuses" and, instead, intercedes for Aaron, Miriam, and the nation of Israel.[97] The people had been delivered from four hundred years of bondage, but they refused to completely trust in the true God. Their hearts were filled with idolatry, yet Moses intercedes for them and asks for forgiveness on their behalf.

Eugene H. Merrill notes Moses's love for the Israelites and his desire for God to show His mercy through forgiveness, "even though they would have to suffer His punishment in some way."[98] Through Moses's ascent, God introduces the concept of forgiveness as He extends mercy toward His people. The encounters with God fuel and empower Moses to proclaim the Lord's name and extol His righteous yet forgiving nature. God used Pharaoh to put Moses in a position of power and authority. He ascended and later revealed God to the Israelites. The glory of the one true God remains unmatched. The image of ascent brings people closer to God, empowering them to lead others to Him just as Moses illustrates.

Ascend to Transformation and Forgiveness

The image of ascent is a movement toward God that transforms individuals so they can share the truth and light of the gospel of Christ with others. A significant aspect of Moses's transformation is his development as an intercessor on behalf of the Israelites. He asks God for forgiveness of their sins, so they can also be in His presence. In response to this intercession, God reveals himself as a merciful and forgiving God: "And he passed in front of Moses, proclaiming, 'The Lord, the Lord, the compassionate and gracious God, slow to anger, abounding in love and faithfulness, maintain love to thousands, and forgiving wickedness, rebellion and sin'" (Exod 34:6). Moses humbly acknowledges the people's stiff-neckedness and asks for God's forgiveness for their wickedness.

Asking for forgiveness remains central to one's ascent to God and spiritual transformation. The significance of forgiveness is seen in Jesus's teaching in the Parable of the

Unmerciful Servant in Matthew 18:21–35, in which a master forgives a large debt that his servant owes him, but shortly afterward, the servant then refuses to forgive a small debt that someone else owes him and throws the debtor in jail (v. 30). When the master hears about this, he is furious and proceeds to throw his servant in jail for his lack of mercy (v. 35). In this parable, Jesus teaches that we must also offer forgiveness to others because God has forgiven all of our sins. The parable asks us to consider whether our transgressions are truly less than someone else's. If the unmerciful servant had recognized the grave state of his own sinfulness, he would have forgiven others who owed him much less.

Unforgiveness, as Diane Swanson explains, puts us in prison, which we will not escape until we choose to forgive from our hearts.[99] Unforgiveness prevents our ability to ascend to God and become transformed. Matthew 18:35 reminds us that we are in prison until we pay back all that we have taken. The only suitable payment is repentance and forgiveness. Paul also teaches us to forgive quickly so that the enemy does not outsmart or take advantage of us (2 Cor 2:10–11).

Shelly Hogan emphasizes the value of letting go of grudges in her soul-healing retreats. Hogan describes the supernatural aspect of forgiving others: "Forgiveness doesn't make sense in the natural. ... Forgiveness is a powerful gift of God to set you free. Forgive the offenses that come; they are stumbling blocks and training blocks."[100] Forgiveness is a supernatural training exercise to grow in godliness. Forgiveness is a muscle that needs to be exercised.

Corrie ten Boom exemplifies the exercise of forgiveness that leads to transformation. She and her immediate family were sent to a concentration camp during World War II for hiding and saving numerous Jewish people in the Netherlands from the Holocaust.[101] Though ten Boom survived Scheveningen prison and, later, the concentration camps at Herzogenbusch-Vught and Ravensbrück, her father and sister died during imprisonment.[102] Her Dutch Protestant upbringing taught her to prioritize others in the spirit of Christian love. She relied on her close relationship with the Lord to lovingly lead and care for victims of the Holocaust. She rose from the depths of hellish torture and used her stories to inspire others to change.

In 1947, at a meeting in Germany, while ten Boom ministered on the subject of forgiveness, she came face-to-face with a former concentration camp guard. Memories of the evil she and her sister Betsie were exposed to immediately flooded her mind. She recounts, "Betsie and I had been arrested for concealing Jews in our home during the Nazi occupation of Holland; this man had been a guard at Ravensbrück concentration camp, where we were sent."[103] The former guard said that Christ had already forgiven him but that he also needed to ask for her forgiveness. ten Boom recounts her struggle as he held out his hand seeking reconciliation:

> It could not have been many seconds that he stood there, hand held out, but to me it seemed hours as I wrestled with the most difficult thing I had ever had to do. … I stood there with the coldness clutching my heart. But forgiveness is not an emotion …. Forgiveness is an act of the will, and the will can function regardless of the temperature of the heart.

> "Jesus, help me!" I prayed silently. "I can lift my hand. I can do that much. You supply the feeling."

> And so woodenly, mechanically, I thrust my hand into the one stretched out to me. And as I did, an incredible thing took place. … This healing warmth seemed to flood my whole being, bringing tears to my eyes.

> … I wish I could say that merciful and charitable

thoughts just naturally flowed from me from then on. But they didn't. If there's one thing I've learned at 80 years of age, it's that I can't store up good feelings and behavior—but only draw them fresh from God each day.[104]

ten Boom's act of forgiveness toward the concentration camp guard marked a profound moment of leadership and obedience, yet it was one that was not limited to a singular moment but numerous moments over a period of time as her years of anger and emotion eventually melted away through her spiritual obedience.

Creative Encounter

Ascending and drawing near to God includes all the senses: the sights, smells, and even tastes that remind you of nearness to God. For some, this is the scent of rain showers, the scent of a well-worn Bible or hymnal, the taste of the bread and juice of communion, the sight of a pink sunrise announcing a new day, or the feeling of peace as it sweeps over you.

Visualize the top of the mountain, the crest of the hill, or a peaceful valley. Maybe you have encountered God near a running stream. What emotions and images best capture your euphoric feeling? What colors and shapes symbolize the transformative moments with God? Imagine nearness to God and express it on a canvas. Capture the thrill of drawing near to God using canvas, paint, and basic outlines. Use simple lines and clean shapes to express the image of ascent.

As an alternate creative expression, think of someone whom you have forgiven. Have you forgiven a friend or family member? Create a canvas that symbolizes the forgiveness in your heart. Collage beautiful traits or hobbies that represent them. This will stand as a declaration of your forgiveness and healing. It may also represent your intercession on their behalf.

Application

Forgiveness, commanded by Scripture, is a vital step in maturing and shaping the spirit. Paul encourages this for the body of Christ: "Be kind and compassionate to one another, forgiving each other, just as in Christ God forgave you" (Eph 4:32), and "bear with each other and forgive one another if any of you has a grievance against someone.

Forgive as the Lord forgave you" (Col 3:13). Forgiving others will require graciousness rather than retribution.[105] It has consequences for both this life and eternity.

Caroline Leaf advocates for cultivating new, healthy thoughts by eliminating bitter, toxic emotions: "Forgiveness enables you to release toxic thoughts of anger, resentment, bitterness, shame, grief, regret, guilt, and hate. It disentangles you from the source of the issue, removing the negative energy from toxic thinking."[106] Neil Anderson offers several helpful insights for practicing forgiveness: "1) Forgiveness is not forgetting. 2) Unforgiveness is hatred. 3) Forgiveness is a choice. 4) Forgiveness is living with the consequences of another's sin. 5) Acknowledge the hurts and the hates. 6) Forgiveness is not a feeling; it is a decision."[107] Anderson also provides a model prayer for forgiveness: "Lord, I release all these people to You and my right to seek revenge. I choose not to hold on to my bitterness and anger, and I ask You to heal my damaged emotions. In Jesus's name, I pray. Amen."[108]

It can be helpful to make a list of offenses and events that need forgiveness. Do not forget to include yourself on this list. Unfortunately, addiction often results in shameful and sorrowful behaviors. As we continue this transforming journey, the full extent of our sinful actions becomes clearer. The list of offenses against us also grows. We must extend the same forgiveness toward ourselves that we offer to others. Offer forgiveness to yourself. Can you truly repay the wrongs? Can you make up for poor judgment, lack of love, or lost time? Will holding a grudge against yourself help anything? Remember this: Even if you start today and try hard, repayment remains impossible. Instead, choose to turn your acts over to God for judgment and release yourself from hatred for your choices. Accept Jesus's forgiveness for your sins.

Does the change and transformation in your life serve as a testimony to others? Seek a platform to reach others. Sharing revelations and transformational experiences strengthens our faith and boosts the faith of others. Recovery testimonies are powerful reminders of God's faithfulness. Just as Moses led others to God, your story can guide others on their recovery journey. Be alert for someone with whom you can share your forgiveness story. Remember, as your relationship with God deepens, you'll gain boldness and clarity to share the love of Jesus. Recognize that your spiritual transformation is even stronger when you share it with others.

As bitterness and unforgiveness are dealt with in our personal lives, the evidence of God restoring and fighting on our behalf will become clear. I often wonder how many times my bitter roots of unforgiveness have kept me from ascending to God. I must remind myself that God will not go back on His Word. If He says to forgive, we must forgive, so the Just Judge will take up our cause (Matt 6:14–15).

CHAPTER 5: IMAGE OF CLEANSING

Introduction

Spiritual growth for a new life is demonstrated through the cleansing and atonement process, exemplified by the image of cleansing proclaimed by John the Baptist. John the Baptist calls both Jews and Gentiles to seek cleansing for the forgiveness of sins. As the forerunner of the Messiah, he preached repentance to "prepare the way of the Lord" (Isa 40:3). His role in biblical history fulfilled another prophetic declaration of the coming Savior. John the Baptist delivers a new message to the Judean people and announces that they must prepare their hearts for the coming of the Savior, which had been foretold for millennia.

John the Baptist

John the Baptist devoted his life to proclaiming the Messiah, and he reinterpreted traditional Jewish purification rituals to foreshadow a new kind of cleansing that would sanctify the heart. Sanctification, according to Evan Howard, is a priority of spiritual formation because it aims us "toward a deepening relationship and an increasing conformity with the wonderful life, message, and mission of Jesus Christ."[109] Sanctification and the pursuit of godliness through Jesus Christ is the ultimate goal of spiritual formation. This pursuit includes cleansing, as illustrated by the life of John the Baptist.

This cleansing, however, differed from the Jewish ceremonial washing conducted under the guidance of the religious authorities of the time, according to Craig Keener.[110] Keener explains that "Jewish people often believed that they were saved by virtue of their descent from Abraham, which constituted them as the chosen people."[111] They believed that their heritage and keeping of the Law sufficiently earned them a place in heaven.

As they maintained ritual purity, they believed they were securing their eternity. The act of baptism also differed from Jewish cleansing rituals, which were self-administered, whereas water baptism involved a baptizer and a baptizee. Expounding on rituals from antiquity, Risto Uro observes: "Other Jewish ritual washings were self-administered, while in John's immersion, there is an agent of the ritual (John or his disciple) and a ritual patient (someone who came to be baptized)."[112]

This ritual cleaning, known as the *mikvah*, entailed ceremonial bathing in a "gathering of water … [including] reservoirs, cisterns, irrigation channels, and stone and wooden vessels."[113] The body of water needed to be deep enough to fully submerge an adult. Benjamin Snyder explains that the Jewish requirement of ritual purity (Lev 11–15; 22; Num 19; Lev 15:31) "ultimately led to the development of the *mikveh* or stepped bath,"[114] which was pervasively utilized throughout Jewish culture: "*Mikva'ot* were so widely dispersed and integral to Jewish life of the Second Temple Period that they have been found in every Jewish archaeological site in the land of Israel and are located in the homes of people from every social class."[115]

John, however, reinterprets the Jewish *mikvah* by incorporating repentance and cleansing from sin through water (Mark 1:4). Don Allen Tennison agrees, claiming that "John is known for being in the wilderness, but while there, he invites all of Israel to a fresh commitment to God through ritual cleansing. ... Spiritual formation as cleansing understands formation to be a form of purification in light of contamination of sin."[116] Baptism was a washing, of sorts, so that one could come near to God.

People responded to the call to be washed of sin. Individuals, families, and crowds repented and were baptized. "Now John also was baptizing at Aenon near Salim, because there was plenty of water, and people were coming and being baptized" (John 3:23). Ithamar Gruenwald examines early Christianity and its rituals, including baptism. His research explores Jewish full immersion for purification, noting that "This implied that full immersion of the whole body could be done there, most likely in accordance with the halakic rulings."[117] Snyder suggests that the baptism offered by John would have repurposed *mikva'ot* for baptism: "The baptisms of the earliest believers would likely have taken place in a *mikveh*. While some New Testament immersions did take place in rivers ... the earliest known baptisteries date to AD 240."[118] Snyder's comments should be compared to scripture, which supports baptizing in bodies of water such as the Ethiopian and Phillip on the journey from Jerusalem to Gaza, "Look, here is water. What can stand in the way of my being baptized?" (Acts 8:37). Additionally, John the Baptizer was at the river, "confessing their sins, they were baptized by him in the Jordan River" (Matt 3:6). Although the preferred method of baptism was immersion, the new disciples were not held to ceremonial practices.

According to the Apostles' writings in the *Didache*, rivers were used for Christian baptisms, or if rivers were not available, water could be poured over the believer's head three times:

> And concerning baptism, baptize this way: Having first said all these things, baptize into the name of the Father, and of the Son, and of the Holy Spirit, in living water. But if you have no living water, baptize into other water; and if you cannot do so in cold water, do so in warm. But if you have neither, pour out water three times upon the head into the name of Father and Son and Holy Spirit. But before the baptism let the baptizer fast, and the baptized, and whoever else can; but you shall order the baptized to fast one or two days before.[119]

This reinterpretation of the *mikvah* and the Jewish tradition of washing in relation to one's birthright challenged the assertion of salvation through heritage. John's message that all needed to repent and be baptized placed "Jewish people on the same terms as pagans."[120] Not surprisingly, John's message angered the religious leaders. The image of cleansing promoted by John the Baptist symbolizes cleansing and purity of the heart rather than trust in tradition and family lineage.

Baptism became transformative when coupled with repentance from sin. The call to repentance, however, was not a new concept. Old Testament prophets had been warning of disaster or destruction for wrongdoing and calling for repentance and fasting to avert God's wrath. Isaiah while prophesying to Judah says, "Wash and make yourselves clean. Take your evil deeds out of my sight; stop doing wrong" (Isa 1:16). Lesley DiFransico states that the repentance that John preached added a new dimension to what the Old Testament prophets called for: It "reflects a similar reorientation of the mind away from sin and wrong behavior. Such a change of mind (μετάνοια, *metanoia*) reflects a reorientation of the will toward obedience to God and a turning (ἐπιστρέφω, *epistrephō*) toward faith in Christ."[121] The Hebrew word, שׁוּב, means: 'go back, return, move back to a place."[122] This is used repeatedly in the Old Testament to denote turning back to God in relation to the prophet's call to repent.

The repentance preached by John calls for true cleansing, a turning away from sin and going a different way, toward the Messiah. The image of cleansing was familiar to John's audience, as they had long practiced ritual purification for cleanliness. Levitical Law states that purity is essential for pleasing God and being in His presence.

Wayne Dehoney summarizes that, after Jesus's death, the act of baptism and cleansing becomes complete in meaning: "Paul states the symbolism of immersion (Rom. 6:3–7) to be the death, burial, and resurrection of Christ and the believer's personal experience of death to sin and resurrection to new life in Christ."[123] Dehoney asserts that new life represents the fulfillment of the ritual cleansing and atonement process: "The NT did not reject the OT concept of clean and unclean but rather reinterpreted it in a new context. It stressed in particular the moral sense of the concept as well as the identification of uncleanness with sin."[124] John the Baptist used this reinterpretation of cleansing to call for repentance of all people. According to James Hastings et al., "The consequences of uncleanness and the methods of purification naturally differed in different races. But in the Jewish religion, uncleanness was always held to disqualify a man for Divine worship and sacrifice."[125] The relationship of sin and ritual impurity is that both keep people from God, and without holiness, none will see God.

In Luke's narrative of John the Baptist, the apostle notes that the crowd, the tax collectors, and the soldiers were inquisitive about the new idea of baptism of repentance for the forgiveness of sins. The people were accustomed to ritual cleansing, which addressed ritual impurity, but the concept of repentance was new. In response to their questions, John teaches on the fruits of repentance, which include sharing what one has, being satisfied with one's wages, refraining from false accusations, and refraining from forcibly taking money from others (3:11-14). The image of cleansing presented by John the Baptist reveals the spiritual growth that is revealed in one's daily life.

Commitment to Cleansing

An ongoing debate exists about whether addiction is inherited or a learned behavior. While a discussion of this debate is outside the scope of this resource, biblical answers that promote health, healing, and positive habits through repentance and spiritual formation apply in either case. The Bible exhorts us to refrain from dwelling on and engaging in sinful behaviors. Addiction calls us to end the pain, both emotional and physical, by any means. Meeting one's needs by any means other than with Jesus is idolatry. This stands against the first and second commandments: "You shall have no other gods before Me," and "you shall not make for yourself a carved image" (Exod 20:3-4). In other words, no other god comes before Jesus, and idolatry has no place in our lives. Sobriety and humility remind us that Jesus paid for our freedom to serve the one true God.

As Paul teaches in Romans 6, once a person has been baptized, they are no longer slaves to sin: "But thanks be to God that, though you used to be slaves to sin, you have come to obey from your heart the pattern of teaching that has now claimed your allegiance. You have been set free from sin and have become slaves to righteousness" (vv. 17-18). The old is gone, and the new has come. Paul's teaching is clear: Baptism brings new life and fellowship with God.

John the Baptist proclaimed the coming of the Deliverer who surpasses all previous sacrifices. Jesus is the final sacrifice for humankind, and all the need for penance and payment is made with His life. He is the atoning sacrifice for every sin forever. Unlike ritual cleansing in the Old Testament, which was repeated, baptism is only done once. We need not deny our sinful behavior or fallen state. Embracing Christ means repentance and forgiveness. A move from denial to acceptance is a leap of faith that Jesus will cleanse, heal, and restore.

Through repentance, we will see good fruit in our lives. This is affirmed in 2 Chronicles 7:14, which states,

"If my people, which are called by my name, shall humble themselves, and pray, and seek my face, and turn from their wicked ways; then will I hear from heaven, and will forgive their sin, and will heal their land." The fruit of forgiveness comes from repenting, cleansing, and submitting our lives to God. God is pleased when our hearts turn toward Him.

Those of us who have struggled with addiction, however, must always be attuned to our tendency to deny our need for repentance or healing. Denial can stand in the way of experiencing the cleansing John the Baptist taught about, and it can cause us to remain enslaved to sin. Wendy Buttacy describes the denial that comes with addiction as "toxic denial," which is defined as "refusing to accept or acknowledge something as reality or fact and acting in a way that reflects that belief."[126] Denial includes downplaying sin or a transgressing situation. Buttacy explains that denial is easier than acknowledging the trauma, loss, or fault because we often feel safer in our brokenness. We have made broken places our familiar places. To avoid God's judgment and experience true freedom, we must invite God to cleanse our hearts and minds from sin and wrongdoing.

I vividly recall sitting in my first NA (Narcotics Anonymous) meeting. After hearing a few people share, I leaned over to my husband and whispered, "I don't belong here with these people. I think we should leave."

He responded, "You are one of these people. You need to be here!" Really? Are the junkie stories and thieving lies also mine? In my mind, the white, middle-class mother didn't seem to fit my stereotype of an addict. In a desire to protect my ego, I denied that I belonged to the addiction community.

Denial has many facets, and sometimes it can be simply a psychological defense mechanism.[127] When denial is due to being defensive and based on emotion, it means that "fully acknowledging addiction-related problems" is "threatening to the individual's ego," and that causes the individual to "misconstrue, reinterpret, or even forget the facts of the case."[128] In other cases, however, denial is not due to one's rejection of the truth to protect their ego. Instead, according to research done by Rinn et al., severe denial results from cognitive problems and lack of insight, the inability to recognize the severity of one's addiction illness:

> Denial is sometimes more of a cognitive failure than an ego defense mechanism. This cognitive failure may consist of diminished capacity for insight, or it may be an inability to integrate readily available information so as to draw an obvious conclusion. It may involve an inability to develop an organized, systematic approach

for searching memory and for searching the environment for evidence of alcoholism, as well as poor discrimination of relevant from nonrelevant evidence. It may be influenced by mental rigidity, concreteness of thought, and poor ability to deal with complexity. Such cognitive deficits are common in alcoholics.

Undoubtedly, the denial displayed by individuals with alcohol and other drug dependencies sometimes has a defensive component. However, a pattern of severe denial in the face of overwhelming evidence of addiction and addiction-related problems is also consistent with a cognitive defect.[129]

In other words, denial is not always a choice nor an unwillingness to acknowledge the truth. Severe cases of denial are often due to cognitive and neurological problems. As a result, the often-used confrontation or intervention is typically not effective in cases that involve lack of insight and cognitive deficits because those individuals do not have the capacity to recognize the state of their own illness.

The treatment options for addiction denial due to cognitive dysfunction include "a structured and paced approach, in which information is presented in small, manageable chunks and reinforced before more information is presented."[130] All addicts, even those who are dealing with cognitive deficits and lack of insight, can absorb a manageable presentation of Jesus and His teachings because the Word of God is effective in changing lives.

Denial, regardless of its cause, can still be quite destructive, according to Charity Anderson, who highlights its consequences: "Denial prevents many people from understanding the toll that their harmful behavior takes on themselves and those they love."[131] She lists several signs and symptoms of addiction denial, including "irritability, being dismissive, blaming others, and appearing in control."[132] Denial harms one's physical health, emotional health, mental health, and spiritual health. Denial has consequences, whether it is fueled by shame, enabled by others, driven by coping mechanisms, or resulting from impaired cognitive functions.

We must remember that those of us who have struggled with substance abuse are not alone. We can find fellowship in groups and communities. We need not deny our sinful behaviors, wanderings, or rebellion. We can admit them and turn to Jesus, who is our covering, and He will hear and redeem us. Jesus himself speaks on the availability of forgiveness: "This is my blood of the covenant, which is poured out for many for the forgiveness of sins" (Matt 26:28). Jesus also points to the nearness of God: "The time has come," he said. "The kingdom of God has come near. Repent and believe the good news!" (Mark 1:14).

Creative Encounter

Consider what dirt and rags you left by the wayside as you experienced cleansing. What image of cleansing portrays your heart transformation? What are examples of your fruit of repentance? Create a project featuring your future as you walk with Jesus. Canvas your move towards God with the promises of new life, health, and relationships. Maybe add some current photos of your support community, family, and mentors. What activities are you enjoying as a result of clean living and clear-mindedness?

By this point, you have likely found your preferred supplies for the creative encounter portion of this resource. I want to encourage you to keep exploring with God. The great thing about creativity is that we can utilize all types of materials. You could use recycled paper or wrappers to symbolize how God has taken the trash of your life and turned it into beauty. Collaging on canvas is an effective way to recycle refuse.

Application

Acknowledging sinful choices, repenting, and aligning our minds to follow Christ increases our awareness of our need for the Savior. How will you commit to ongoing cleansing? A good starting point is to admit to past situations that led to sin and reflect on them. Elmer L. Towns encourages the spiritual discipline of fasting to make us aware of the desires that drive our behaviors. He also notes how the ego, or self-esteem, can negatively influence behavior. When we desire protection, he explains, "we feel threatened by losing life's basic necessities."[25] When we want to be exalted, "we feel embarrassed or feel that others minimize us."[133] When we want to be accepted, "we are alienated or frozen out of the group."[134] When we want respect, "we feel threatened because of criticism or direct attacks."[135] Towns suggests fasting for revelation and insight into challenging situations. This discipline encourages self-reflection and honest examination of oneself. A self-assessment could identify triggers of sinful behaviors that may be as simple as feelings of hunger, anger, or loneliness. If we recognize that our past tendencies have included overindulgence, walking in fear, gossiping, lying, or committing other sins, be wise and attentive! We know the enemy of our souls plays old records, luring us into destructive paths.

In addition to fasting, have you followed the example of Jesus and been baptized? The image of cleansing is for all, not just an elite group. We all need the cleansing that comes with immersion and the confession of a changed life. According to the Assemblies of God fundamental truths, "The ordinance of baptism by immersion is commanded by the Scriptures. All who repent and believe in Christ as Savior and Lord are to be baptized. Thus they declare to the world that they have died with Christ and that they also have been raised with Him to walk in newness of life."[136] Having our hearts cleansed and showing the community that we are new creations is the wonderful image of cleansing that John the Baptist embodies.

How will you walk into freedom? What safeguards do you have in your life, such as a supportive community, family, and mentors, to assist in your new walk? Sobriety happens in a community, so we must intentionally plan for a new supportive lifestyle.

CHAPTER 6: IMAGE OF SERVANTHOOD

Introduction

Scripture reveals Jesus as the perfect example of the Servant who fulfilled prophecies, obeyed the Father's will, and is the salvation of humanity. The image of His servanthood, such as Jesus humbly washing the disciples' feet in John 13, is revealed throughout His life and is completely realized at the Ascension. The Apostle Paul also refers to His servanthood in Philippians 2:5-11, which describes Jesus as humble and obedient even to death. Jesus encourages His followers to serve in the same way, with perfect submission and obedience to His Father, unconcerned with personal gain. Jesus's servanthood is reflected in selfless surrender to God. He came to do the will of the Father.

Jesus, the Image of Servanthood

Jesus fulfills the prophecy of the Suffering Servant in Isaiah 53. The Redeemer served all of humanity by restoring humankind to God. He intercedes for and bears the sins of humankind. He is the prophesied Messiah, the Chosen One. Martin Manser describes servanthood as "the state of being the servant of others, especially of God. Scripture stresses the privileges and responsibilities of being a servant of God and points to Jesus Christ as the model of servanthood."[137] Servanthood also "renders service" to others.[138] Fulfilling the Father's will and going to the cross as the New Covenant sacrifice was Jesus's sole focus and responsibility. Additionally, He served humanity through healing and restoring physical bodies, providing food for the crowds, and teaching the underprivileged and the marginalized.

The Jewish people eagerly awaited the Messiah, but when He arrived, He did not meet their expectations. Nijay K.

Gupta describes what the people had been hoping for, which is that the "Messiah would bring the chaotic world back under the harmonious care of the one God. One emphasis is the dialectic role played by the Messiah—on the one hand as the leader of Israel, and, on the other, as an agent that would bring unity and peace to all creatures under the Lord's sovereign authority."[139] Despite fulfilling more than three hundred prophecies, Jesus received no welcome from the Jewish people.

Throughout His earthly encounters, Jesus seeks to reveal His Father. He appears harsh to the religious but is gentle and compassionate toward those who seek truth. Jesus serves not only in obedience, according to Paul, but He emptied himself, taking on the form of a servant, and was made in the likeness of humankind: "And being found in the appearance as a man, he humbled himself by becoming obedient to death, even death on a cross!" (Phil 2:7-8). Paul exhorts followers of Christ to adopt the same obedient mindset as Jesus Christ. Commenting on how Jesus put others first, Warren W. Wiersbe remarks, "Paul traces the steps in the humiliation of Christ: (1) He emptied Himself, laying aside the independent use of His own attributes as God; (2) He permanently became a human, in a sinless physical body; (3) He used that body to be a servant; (4) He took that body to the cross and willingly died."[140] Although we may never die a brutal death for the gospel, we are all called to live out humble servanthood, releasing our selfish desires and taking on the attributes of God.

Robert P. Lightner explains the truth of divinity and humanity described by the Apostle Paul in Philippians 2, which refers to Jesus laying down His divine nature to become human in the most selfless servant posture: "No better example of humiliation and a selfless attitude for believers to follow could possibly be given than that of Christ. With this example before them, the saints at Philippi should be 'like-minded' (v. 2) and live humbly before their God and each other."[141] Paul uses this illustration to point the Philippian believers to become like servants to one another: "Instead of concentrating on self, each believer should be concerned for the interests of others in the household of faith (cf. Rom. 12:10). Preoccupation with oneself is sin."[142] Paul does not go so far as to say that selfishness is sin; however, the attributes of God, which Jesus exemplified, include selfless and abundant giving of himself.

James Swanson points out the unbiased compassion and "disinterested benevolence" of Jesus, which sought the welfare of others without seeking anything in return for himself.[143] Jesus made himself nothing—humble, submissive, and concerned for the welfare of others—and gave His life for those who would follow Him. He sought out the marginalized and despised, such as the Samaritan woman, so that they would know Him (John 4). He exemplifies servanthood by addressing others' needs while guiding them toward a complete understanding of God.

In Matthew 20:26–28, Jesus offers a new perspective on servanthood and leadership in response to a mother's request that her sons sit and rule with Him. He points out that pagan rulers exercise excessive authority over the people, but His disciples are not to behave that way. Rather, as He teaches, His disciples are to serve others: "Whoever wants to become great among you must be your servant, and whoever wants to be first must be your slave—just as the Son of Man did not come to be served, but to serve, and to give his life as a ransom for many" (vv. 26–28). The drastic change that Jesus demands here, according to Craig Keener, was shocking: "Inverting the role of master and slave was radical anywhere in antiquity; even the few masters who believed that slaves were theoretically equals did not go as far as Jesus goes here."[144] In this teaching, Jesus redefines greatness as servanthood.

Jesus not only describes the nature of servanthood through rhetorical arguments, but He also illustrates it through action. John 13:1–17 recounts how Jesus washed the disciples' feet. When Peter hesitates because he does not want Jesus to take on the lowly role of a servant in washing his feet, Jesus firmly responds: "Unless I wash you, you have no part with me" (v. 8). With this statement, Jesus clarifies His identity. Jesus then admonishes His disciples to follow His example: "Now that I, your Lord and Teacher, have washed your feet, you also should wash one another's feet. I have set you an example that you should do as I have done for you. Very truly I tell you, no servant is greater than his master, nor is a messenger greater than the one who sent him. Now that you know these things, you will be blessed if you do them" (John 13:14-17).

D. R. Wood comments on the necessity and meaning of foot washing in the Ancient Near East: "The necessity to wash the feet, for comfort and cleanliness, resulted from the dusty roads, and foot washing was a sign of hospitality."[145] Eugene E. Carpenter notes that this task was typically performed by the household servants.[146] This act of Jesus conveys an important message to His disciples, which was to "come to serve and give His life as a ransom for others."[147] Through foot washing, Jesus demonstrated what He meant when He told His disciples to avoid lording authority over others and, instead, be like Him, a servant or, in the Greek, δοῦλος (Mark 10:43-45).

Martin Manser notes that the concept of servanthood, as illustrated by Jesus, is woven throughout the Gospels:

As [a] servant ... Jesus Christ laid aside his majesty to serve humanity. His death is the supreme example of his servanthood: the fulfilling of the will of God, his Father. The prophets speak of the Messiah as a servant (Matt 12:17-21). ... Jesus Christ describes himself as a servant (Luke 22:27). ... Jesus Christ acts as a servant, by coming to dwell among humanity as a man (Phil 2:6-7) ... by obeying God's will (John 4:34) ... by ministering to his disciples (John 13:1-17), by dying on the cross (Matt 20:28).[148]

Scripture reveals Jesus as the ultimate image of a servant who fulfilled prophecies, was obedient to the Father's will, and is the salvation of humankind. The servant Jesus Christ is seen throughout the history of redemption and is completely realized at the Ascension.

Humble Servanthood

Just like Jesus, obedient servants sacrifice their own preferences in submission to God for the sake of bringing the gospel to others. Servanthood today can take many different forms. Community leaders and volunteers can engage in grassroots operations on the local level, which can include organizations such as food banks, diaper banks, refugee services, homeless shelters, Boys and Girls Club, community gardens, libraries, and church operations, among others. Numerous opportunities exist for serving one's own local community.

Research shows that people personally benefit when they help others. While Jesus came to serve others regardless of benefit to himself, God has created our bodies to respond positively to serving others. Self-sacrificial acts, such as helping, have been shown to reduce rates of depression, increase longevity, enhance overall physical and mental health, and improve overall happiness over a person's lifetime.[149] Depression, anxiety, and stress are physical responses that may be mitigated through serving others, social connection, and acts of kindness. Research presented by David Cregg and Jennifer Cheavens reports that greater well-being is associated with performing acts of kindness than it is with keeping thought records or planning social activities. Cregg and Cheavens state, "In this study, we demonstrated that performing acts of kindness promotes social connection, a construct that is a key predictor of both well-being and recovery from anxiety and depressive disorders."[150] Likewise, their research also shows that those who tend to primarily focus on themselves and don't engage in helping others tend to suffer more "emotional distress and impaired social functioning."[151] Cregg and Cheavens define acts of kindness as meaning either big or small things done to benefit another with some expense (either in time or resources) to oneself. Their research, which involved having participants perform three acts of kindness each day for two days out of the week demonstrated tangible, positive results in reducing stress, anxiety, and depression.[152]

In addition, service to others also promotes personal health. A published study from Michael J. Poulin et al. reveal the health benefits associated with social interaction and helping behavior: "Positive health outcomes include reduced mortality ... because [helping others] buffers the association between stress and mortality."[153] The research also indicates that those who do not help others but are exposed to stress experience a 30 percent increased mortality risk.[154] Research supports what Jesus modeled and taught His followers: Serving is beneficial both for the person who serves and those who receive that help.

Humble service not only reveals the love of the Father, but it also fulfills the law of God. Paul teaches this in Galatians 5:13-14, stating, "You, my brothers and sisters, were called to be free. But do not use your freedom to indulge the flesh; rather, serve one another humbly in love. For the entire law is fulfilled in keeping this one command: 'Love your neighbor as yourself.'" In other words, serving others has not only physical and mental health benefits; it also has profound spiritual implications.

Opportunities to serve abound in both local and distant locations, as well as in formal and informal settings. Serving others can be accomplished in various ways, depending on one's skills and availability. Volunteers can serve others on a seasonal basis, such as during a Christmas toy drive or handing out Thanksgiving dinners through a local food pantry, or on a more routine basis, such as being a nursery volunteer at church. Cold season service includes participating in coat and blanket drives for a homeless shelter or serving at a soup kitchen. In areas with hot weather, cooling shelters may need volunteers. Serving others can even be the focus of one's vocation.

Serving others can also be done through part-time or full-time employment with organizations dedicated to community service. Convoy of Hope, for example, feeds hundreds of thousands of children around the world, performs community outreaches, and provides disaster relief both in the United States and abroad.[155] For over thirty years, the nonprofit humanitarian organization has provided $3.5 billion in relief supplies worldwide.[156] The Missouri-based ministry, which began in response to one man's story of poverty and hunger, has grown into an international relief agency. Convoy of Hope, with its white-and-red trailers and semi-trucks, addresses needs in the following areas: children's feeding programs, disaster relief (both in the U.S. and around the world), agriculture, women's empowerment, and community engagement events. Convoy of Hope provides school meals for poverty-stricken children in thirty-nine countries. The school feeding program serves 639,000 children through personalized nutrition, assessments, multivitamin supplementation, and prenatal/postnatal nutrition. In addition, Convoy also facilitates community engagement events in various places in the United States, including both rural and urban areas, an initiative that brings services to the needy, such as haircuts, school backpacks, eye testing, and hearing testing. Convoy also provides opportunities for prayer, a job fair, help with resumes, and many other needs. Convoy of Hope uses volunteers from local churches and nonprofits to invest in the local community, while also pointing outreach attendees to the local church to fulfill the ongoing spiritual needs of the people.[157]

Another ministry organization making a difference in the world is Project Rescue, an international ministry saving women and children from sexual traffickers. The ministry was birthed in the hearts of David and Beth Grant in India's red-light district. Since its inception in 1997, the ministry has expanded from India into fifteen other countries and provinces. Serving the prostitutes and their at-risk children is at the heart of the ministry. In addition to providing shelter and the gospel of Jesus to the workers and children, Project Rescue also maintains schools to educate, house, and feed children. These residential programs provide victims and their children the necessary stability and Christ-centered healing they need to rebuild their lives.[158] The influence of Project Rescue extends beyond the frailty and brokenness of the individual's heart. Prevention, intervention, and restoration bring hope, healing, and salvation to each survivor. The servant-hearted leaders and staff of Project Rescue present a real-time example of Jesus.

Other examples of service to others is illustrated by Rebecca Shults, who brings healing through the creative arts to victims whose voices have been silenced. Shults, the founder and creator of the Healing Arts Method, uses creative activities, including drama, journaling, drawing, sculpting, and other creative activities with survivors. Her principles include "expression, cognition, co-creation, safe spaces, unconditional positive regard, and process over product," which provide an opportunity for trauma survivors to experience emotional healing and growth.[159]

As these three examples show, in the kingdom of God, plenty of opportunities exist to practice compassion for the poor, the needy, victims of abuse, the homeless, and others who have experienced great hardship. Expressing love by showing kindness, volunteering, and sharing the story of Jesus with those who are hurting demonstrates love to neighbors. What we must remember is that our former membership in the addiction community does not prevent us from serving others. If anything, our experiences with addiction can make us more understanding and more compassionate.

Robert L. Woodson agrees. He documents community efforts led by recovering addicts, former homeless, and post-poverty people, writing, "Often, they themselves once struggled with the very vices they now are helping others overcome. They once were menaces to society but now are ministers and witnesses."[160] Our history doesn't dismiss us from service for the Kingdom. In fact, the opposite is true. Those of us who have overcome are well-equipped to give their testimony and lend a hand to others.

Creative Encounter

Jesus knew the plan and purpose for His life. Likewise, we need to seek God and find the purpose that God has for us. Think about a small and simple task that you can do to serve another person. Find images that inspire you to serve others. Collage the canvas with a collection of servant-hearted images or other-focused images. Although you may not have the opportunity to participate (yet) in the actions, create a canvas with ideas of serving others. If you have ever desired to serve on a mission or work in a parachurch organization, now is the time to express your heart for service. Be sure to include the skills or supplies needed for the mission or service project. Let yourself imagine and explore all the what-ifs of service ideas.

Don't shy away from this time of creativity with God. He may add a new experience to your spirit. He may call you into a place of low regard. Take the time during this creative encounter to listen to the Holy Spirit. Listen obediently to what the Spirit is saying to you about servanthood.

Application

Addiction promotes a selfish lifestyle. The years spent in self-centeredness can be hard to shake off. Thankfully, receiving Jesus Christ as your Savior can reverse years of selfishness and transform one's life. And discussed earlier, serving others will bring health and wholeness to us. When submitted to God, our talents, skills, and abilities offer powerful ways to serve others. How can you make a gift of yourself? Are you artistic? Mechanical? Tech-savvy? Caring? Or good at problem-solving? Put your talent to good use by serving others in big or small meaningful ways.

In the grand scheme of things, Christ's witnesses are to share the gospel of Jesus with the world. Christians must avoid distractions and keep their focus heavenward. We must not be dissuaded by the world and the success it promises. As Christians, how do we define success? Is it money, status, achievement, or physical beauty? Kyle Idleman reminds Christians to define success as the Bible does: "And so now, we still care about success, but we define it very differently. He has become our purpose. We live for serving him, for knowing him, for pleasing him. That's how we define success."[161] The addiction community keeps their attention and focus off themselves and on Christ through serving one another.

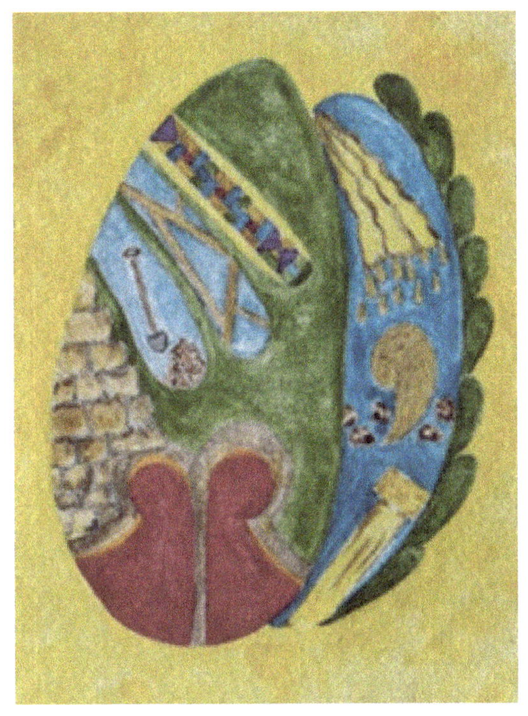

CHAPTER 7: IMAGE OF WITNESS

Introduction

The martyred Stephen serves as a weighty image of witness and the empowering presence of the Holy Spirit amid the threat of death. Stephen served in various capacities, was wise and knowledgeable, was filled with the Holy Spirit, and was bold. He is the first documented non-apostle with signs and miracles attributed to him. He also delivered the longest recorded sermon by a New Testament disciple (Acts 7:2-53) and faithfully served the Grecian widows as one of the seven helpers chosen by the disciples after complaints of unfair treatment arose between the Grecian and Hebrew Jews (6:1-6). Stephen modeled a life of Christian ministry, Spirit empowerment, and the courage to stand up for his faith, even in the face of death.

Stephen

Jesus sent His Spirit to fill the Church so believers can proclaim the gospel to the entire world. He instructed His disciples that they would "receive power when the Holy Spirit comes on you; and you will be my witnesses in Jerusalem, and in all Judea and Samaria, and to the ends of the earth" (Acts 1:8). When they received the Spirit, they became a witness (μάρτυς,), a person who "testifies."[162] Stanley M. Horton points to the power that comes only through the work of the Holy Spirit, who gives believers the "anointing and gifts of the Holy Spirit," so they do not have to rely upon human wisdom.[163] The image of the witness serves as a powerful reminder to live and die filled with the Spirit, without living in fear.[164]

Stephen served the Early Church in a variety of roles. He not only served the widows, but he also "performed great wonders and signs among the people" (Acts 6:8). Wave

Nunnally observes that the diversity of Stephen's ministry offers a helpful example to believers and ministers today, who often tend to specialize in certain types of ministries, resulting in a mentality of elitism, which is neither biblical nor Jesus-centered: "Although [Stephen] was chosen to serve the needy, he is not limited to this facet of ministry. Christians today should avoid the 'specialization' mentality that plagues the rest of the world and put themselves at God's disposal to be used as He needs us."[165] Serving wherever we are needed requires a sensitivity to the Spirit and a life of grace and truth.

Stephen was full of "grace and truth," and Horton notes that the "Holy Spirit worked through Stephen because Stephen reflected the character of Jesus."[166] The leaders of the Jewish people came against Stephen, but they could not stand up to the wisdom the Spirit gave him as he spoke. The wisdom or σοφία that Stephen had is "the capacity to understand and, as a result, to act wisely and prudently."[167] Stephen received godly wisdom to proclaim truth in the face of immense stress.

Stephen was not only given wisdom by the Spirit, but he also cultivated it. Stephen was knowledgeable in the Torah and Israel's history. He recounted the patriarchs and the entire narrative from Abraham through the Messiah. As Stephen performed signs and wonders, members of the Synagogue of the Freedmen began to challenge him, but Stephen was prepared for the debates, armed with the wisdom he had been given by the Spirit (Acts 6:8 10). This demonstration of wisdom, however, angered his challengers, who began to plot ways to bring about his downfall: "They then secretly persuaded some men to say, 'We have heard Stephen speak blasphemous words against Moses and against God.' So, they stirred up the people and the elders and the teachers of the law. They seized Stephen and brought him before the Sanhedrin" (vv. 11–12) for a trial.

In Acts 7:1, the High Priest asks whether the charges against Stephen are accurate. If convicted, Stephen would certainly die. Instead of defending himself, however, Stephen takes the opportunity to preach the longest recorded sermon by a disciple. Stephen begins with Abraham, proceeds to the patriarchs, and recounts the history of Moses, the Law, and the Tabernacle as he stands before the Sanhedrin. Knowing that the death penalty was looming over him, he boldly challenged his audience and used this platform to share redemptive history to effectively communicate and "chide the people of God for their disobedience and unresponsiveness, and to call for repentance and covenant faithfulness."[168] Not surprisingly, the members of the Sanhedrin were outraged by Stephen's rebuke.

What happens next is a subject of debate among scholars. John Polhill notes that "scholars are divided as to whether Stephen was formally sentenced to stoning ... or whether he died by mob violence. ... What began as a formal trial deteriorated into a lynch mob, so furious were the Jewish leaders at Stephen's words."[169] The text implies that mob violence took Stephen's life because, according to Wave Nunnally, the stoning did not follow normal protocol. He notes, "Now the previously judicial situation has turned into mob violence. There is no report of a vote taken, and the normal procedure for handling a capital case according to Pharisaic law is no longer followed (similar to what happened to Jesus)."[170]

Stephen led the way to martyrdom, and many others would follow, refusing to be silenced for their faith. Stefana Dan Laing observes that the meaning of martyr did not hold the modern definition: "In the Septuagint this term rarely denotes one killed for his or her testimony, although a case may perhaps be made thematically in reference to prophetic proclamation."[171] According to D.A. Carson, "The word martyr didn't take on the idea of giving witness by dying for your faith until later in the Christian era."[172] Bearing witness to Christ includes remaining faithful to the teachings found in Scripture. Paul Hartog argues that in recent centuries, a martyr refers to someone who prefers to die for their religious convictions rather than abandon them; however, he notes that the early Greeks used the term to refer to a witness with the "specifically legal connotation as one who testifies before a court, … a person who suffers death for his or her faith or convictions."[173] Martyrs, then, according to Hartog serve as witnesses to "their commitment [and] to their beliefs at the cost of their lives."[174] Eugene Carpenter clarifies that the English word *martyr* comes from "the Greek word *martus* … since one who witnesses for his or her faith in Christ would often die for making that testimony."[175] John the Baptist became the first Christian witness and martyr for proclaiming Herod's sins. Stephen, however, was the first martyr for the Church.

Wayne Dehoney notes that Stephen was a layman, and that his "death did not destroy his witness. The centuries to follow would reveal that the blood of martyrs is the seed of the church."[176] The account of the martyred Stephen serves as a substantial image of witness, encouraging boldness for spiritual development. Believers can reflect on the empowering presence of the Holy Spirit and the strength provided to those who testify about Christ. The image of the witness serves as a powerful reminder to live and die filled with the Spirit.

Historically, the Christian faith has grown in response to

persecution and oppression. Stephen's life had several key outcomes for the Kingdom's expansion. The first is that his life and story illustrated that God is for all and is not exclusive to the Israelites. Nunnally explains how Stephen's speech opened the door to inclusiveness: Stephen is "the first in Acts to suggest that the presence of God is not limited to the temple or even to the land of Israel. In this, he lays the groundwork for others after him to conclude that a relationship with God is not limited to the Jews, but is available to all, irrespective of geography or ethnicity."[177] Secondly, the Stephen account introduces Saul, who, at the time, persecuted the early Christians but later becomes a significant church planter, missionary, and leader. Stephen's story also reveals how the Church dispersed geographically. The spread of the gospel of Jesus Christ springs from the witnesses who lived and died for the message.

Lastly, Stephen's story encourages believers to be courageous, seek the filling of the Spirit, and to not fear failure. As Horton encourages, the Holy Spirit has come to ensure that failure is not an option: "Don't wait for ideal conditions before spreading the gospel to the nations. This age is characterized by wars, rumors of wars, famines, and earthquakes. … As his witnesses, believers must go out and spread the gospel to all nations in the midst of all the natural calamities and political upheavals, regardless of the cost."[178]

This is only possible, however, as the power of the Holy Spirit is poured out and received.

Just as Peter preached in Acts 2:38, the Holy Spirit remains available to those who receive the Savior and invite the Holy Spirit to inhabit them: "Repent and be baptized, every one of you, in the name of Jesus Christ for the forgiveness of your sins. And you will receive the gift of the Holy Spirit. The promise is for you and your children and for all who are far off—for all whom the Lord our God will call." The empowerment and boldness that the Holy Spirit offers us to witness to others remains unparalleled. As Horton rightly concludes, "The call to be His witnesses then makes us Spirit-empowered ambassadors whose lives and ministries are extensions of the Spirit-empowered life and ministry of Jesus."[179]

Bearing witness to Jesus at the end of his life, Stephen prayed for his accusers, including Saul, who was in the crowd (Acts 7:57-60). Stephen followed Christ's example in his last moments. Robert Brandt and Zenas Bicket boldly remind Christians to remain focused on eternal values rather than temporal concerns: "How should we react to persecution and abuse? Stephen's prayer expressed two concerns: the destination of his spirit and the welfare of his enemies. Jesus had the same concern a few months earlier while dying at the hands of evil men."[180] In addition,

Brandt and Bicket maintain that Steven continues to reveal a forgiving heart like Jesus: "In humble response to the horrible violence of which he was now the victim, he displayed no hint of retaliation in his redeemed spirit. There was only compassion and tender concern for those who in the next instant would snuff out his life."[181][20] We must be emboldened and spread Jesus's message, acknowledging that we may ultimately be called to sacrifice our lives for Him. How can individuals become authentic, living witnesses for Christ? The image of a witness serves as a powerful call to abandon the world, fear, and apprehension while wholeheartedly following Jesus.

Authentic Reflection of Christ

Gone are the days of going door-to-door to distribute witnessing tracts. Cultural changes in society, along with the widespread use of social media, have changed how we witness, yet relational evangelism, one in which the believer builds meaningful relationships with those around them, remains the most effective and powerful form of sharing the gospel. Sharing one's faith should not be a terrifying or anxiety-laden activity. Instead, it should flow naturally as the believer walks daily in the overflow of joy and peace that they experience in everyday situations and challenges. David Neyland Sumarauw speaks of the importance of living out daily expressions of faith in Christ: "Living testimony is one of the most effective methods of evangelism. It is not only witnessing the message of the Gospel delivered orally, but the lifestyle and deeds in daily life. Being the salt and light of the world in terms of acts of love, holiness and obedience to God becomes the light of truth that emanates from his life."[182] Believers have many opportunities to reflect Christ, whether in friendships at work, in the neighborhood, in the family, at school, and in other community activities.

Johannes Reimer coined the term "frangelism" to describe personal evangelism among friends, relatives, associates, and neighbors.[183] Reimer explains that frangelism is based on the Early Church model used by the apostles, who saw the rapid spread of the gospel. Witnessing in household and familial settings was the preferred method of witnessing for the Early Church, since, as Allen C. Myers, notes, ancient households were often quite large with extended family and could "comprise as many as five generations."[184] Reimer notes that sharing Jesus with family and close relations should be a natural, ongoing, daily activity through casual conversations and lived experiences with the people who remain closest to each other.[185]

Beyond one's family, however, Richard Oliver notes that all work, whether in a retail store, an office, a construction site, or elsewhere, is a divine opportunity to witness for

Christ. The Apostle Paul demonstrated this by working in the marketplace as a tentmaker. Oliver calls Paul's approach as having a "covocational attitude," which "builds on the foundation of seeing one's set of vocations as working together to serve God and His purposes and provides healthy motivation to persist in that service."[186] Paul exemplifies this by working in the marketplace with the purpose of being a witness: "During his initial time in Corinth, Paul works at tentmaking, witnesses to customers as the opportunity arises, and reasons in the synagogue every sabbath" (Acts 18:4).[187] We can use our vocational position as an opportunity to share Jesus every day.

Another way to be a witness to others is in our use of social media, which extends beyond the neighborhood into global society. There are both pros and cons to this method. The Internet has enabled many more people to be reached with the gospel, but the praxis of making disciples through digitalization methods remains challenging. Victor Ogunsola advocates for digital discipleship, citing the many in-person limitations in violent areas, disruptions to community life, and other safety concerns that prevent gatherings: "Online libraries, podcasts, and video content provide easy access to biblical teachings and theological discussions. … By embracing digital tools, missionaries can continue their vital work of spreading the gospel and supporting the faithful even in the most challenging circumstances."[188] Additionally, any believer can make use of digital evangelism, and it does not have to be time-consuming. One can simply use their social media as a source of encouragement and prayer for others and reaching out to friends in need.

Another important but often overlooked way to share Christ, according to Yakubu Jakada, is by spending time with older adults and senior citizens. Jakada notes that ministries often ignore outreach to older adults, leaving an important population, many of whom are home bound, without the gospel. Jakada notes that believers who reach out to older adults should be "born again and Spirit-filled, love people, a good listener, patient, understand issues related to old age, compassionate, a disciple maker, respectful, and availability for visitation."[189]

David Neyland Sumarauw reminds us that evangelism and witnessing for Christ is how the church grows. Effective evangelism is not knocking on strangers' doors handing out tracts. It's a natural outcome of developing meaningful relationships with others and "finding people in need, building friendships, involving others, clearing up misunderstandings, reconstructing the understanding and trust, restoring the wrong way of life, and preaching Jesus as Messiah."[190]

Creative Encounter

For this encounter, ask the Holy Spirit to give you an idea of a platform you can use to witness. Examples include a business venture or work-related activities, a needy situation where a Jesus testimony could help, family outings to share about Jesus, or even a neighborhood activity. Use magazines or printed advertisements as elements to collage onto your canvas.

Add bold color that evokes feelings of spiritual empowerment. What does being full of grace and God's power look like in your recovery journey? An alternate project would be to select a shape that represents you and draw yourself witnessing for Christ. Where do you work, live, and socialize? Capture these places on canvas as places to witness to others about Jesus.

Application

Spiritual development is essential for witnessing. You can prepare to defend the hope of the Lord Jesus. Be sure to practice your testimony by writing and rehearsing your story. How are you studying, learning, and growing in godliness? With the availability of online classes and courses, as well as traditional home groups, friend groups, and step programs, there are numerous high-quality opportunities to lean into fellowship. Ask the Lord to guide you in finding a group to belong to for accountability, to give your testimony, and to grow in godliness. Make learning and sharing a consistent part of your routine.

Have you been filled and continuously refilled with the power of the Holy Spirit? What habits of transformation and spiritual training are you submitting to? Who are you regularly witnessing to in your life and work? What does it look like to be full of grace and God's power? What platform do you stand on as a result of sobriety? With whom can you share your recovery journey? Ask and receive the fullness of the Holy Spirit for the power to share the gospel. A witness is knowledgeable, service-hearted, and filled with the Holy Spirit. Imagine that the fear of others is no longer in your way. Who would you share Jesus with? Now imagine the most difficult person accepting Jesus. Would this possibility give you hope and purpose to keep sharing and witnessing?

Chapter 8: Image of Encounter

Introduction

Prior to becoming a church planter and missionary, Saul, later referred to as the Apostle Paul, terrorized followers of Christ. Luke first introduces Saul during the tragic stoning of Stephen (Acts 7:54-60) and then describes him as going house to house, arresting believers and throwing them into prison (8:3). As Saul continued his campaign of terror, journeying on the road to Damascus, a light from heaven suddenly "flashed around him. He fell to the ground and heard a voice say to him, 'Saul, Saul, why do you persecute me?' 'Who are you, Lord?' Saul asked. 'I am Jesus, whom you are persecuting,' he replied. 'Now get up and go into the city, and you will be told what you must do'" (Acts 9:3-6). Saul experiences an encounter with Jesus, a sudden and unexpected confrontation that stops him cold in his tracks. He is blinded for three days by the encounter, until Ananias obeys a word from the Lord to go pray for the restoration of Saul's sight and the baptism in the Holy Spirit (vv. 10–18).

The Nature of Encounters with God

A Dramatic Encounter

The life-changing meeting with Jesus on the road to Damascus epitomizes the image of encounter. In Acts 22:3-5, after he had been arrested by Jewish leaders for preaching the gospel to Gentiles, Saul stands before a crowd to give his testimony about his Damascus Road experience and describes himself prior to his transformation:

> I am a Jew, born in Tarsus of Cilicia, but brought
> up in this city. I studied under Gamaliel and was

thoroughly trained in the law of our ancestors. I was just as zealous for God as any of you are today. I persecuted the followers of this Way to their death, arresting both men and women and throwing them into prison, as the high priest and all the Council can themselves testify. I even obtained letters from them to their associates in Damascus and went there to bring these people as prisoners to Jerusalem to be punished.

Although Saul had been a murderer, persecuting Christians and causing chaos in their lives, he met Jesus and was filled with the Holy Spirit, who empowered him to witness for God. The Holy Spirit is the agent through which adversity and challenges are overcome.

When Jesus encounters Saul on the road to Damascus, Saul falls to the ground (Acts 9:4). Nunnally suggests that Saul's falling "was a typical oriental practice, and constituted a voluntary display of humility, respect, and sometimes worship usually referred to as 'prostration.'"[191] However, Craig Keener asserts that Saul's response provides a different perspective of the encounter: "In the Old Testament and Jewish literature, people often fell to the ground when confronted with divine or angelic revelations (e.g., Ezek 1:28; Dan 8:17). Usually, the revealer then commands the person to stand (e.g., Ezek 2:1; Dan 8:18); the lack of such instruction here likely suggests that Saul's behavior is not an object of divine favor."[192] Keener adds that God can intervene to convert a persecutor, which appears to be the case with Saul.[193] Regardless of Saul's state of mind during the encounter, he shows humility as he acknowledges the Lord.

The Lord then uses Ananias to confirm Saul's calling, saying to Ananias, "Go! This man is my chosen instrument to proclaim my name to the Gentiles and their kings and to the people of Israel. I will show him how much he must suffer for my name" (Acts 9:15-16). Ananias obeys God, finds Saul, and places his hands upon him, saying, "Brother Saul, the Lord—Jesus, who appeared to you on the road as you were coming here—has sent me so that you may see again and be filled with the Holy Spirit" (v. 17). At that moment, the scales fall from Saul's eyes and he receives the baptism in the Holy Spirit (v. 18). F. F. Bruce describes this infilling as giving Saul "indispensable qualification for the prophetic and apostolic service," which endows him "with heavenly power."[194] Once he finishes his job of speaking God's call for Saul, Ananias leaves the story as quickly as he had entered it.[195]

As Nunnally points out, Jesus was expanding Saul's "concepts of God and His Kingdom."[196] The evangelistic ministry to the nations is beginning in this event. The kingdom of God is for all humankind; Jews and Gentiles are to hear of the salvation of Jesus Christ. Saul receives his call to the Gentiles, a charge to proclaim the message of repentance, forgiveness, and salvation as God's direction for his assignments. Later he receives the promise of future revelations and protection for his journeys (23:11). The encounter with Jesus revealed to Saul that God desired all to worship Him, and he would be an agent of this message to the Gentiles.

The Damascus Road encounter is not the only encounter Paul experiences. Other encounters include being caught up in the third heaven (2 Cor 12), escaping angry mobs (Acts 13:49–52, 22:19–24), and a visitation by an angel who offers direction and comfort (27:23). Each encounter serves as a fresh reminder of Paul's purpose and provision. Acts 22:17 describes one encounter with the Lord in which Paul prays at the temple and falls into an ecstatic trance.[197] The Lord then instructs him to quickly leave Jerusalem because Paul's testimony would be rejected due to his history of persecution; instead, he is to go far away to evangelize the Gentiles (vv. 17–21).

Elsewhere, Paul describes an encounter with an angel: "Last night an angel of the God to whom I belong and whom I serve stood beside me and said, 'Do not be afraid,

Paul'" (27:24). The angel reassures Paul and calms his fears of being lost at sea on his way to stand trial in Rome before Caesar. This encounter emboldens Paul to encourage the ship crew. This long and dangerous journey ends successfully, with Paul and the entire crew reaching shore.

A Low-Key but Equally Life-Changing Encounter

God uses common activities as well as dramatic events to encounter His people. Such is the story of the Samaritan woman at the well as documented by John. She was doing the daily, mundane chore of getting water when an unexpected and life-changing interaction with Jesus occured: "It was about noon. When a Samaritan woman came to draw water, Jesus said to her, 'Will you give me a drink?'" (John 4:6–7). Colin Kruse notes that the timing of this interaction, around noon, is notable and strange because it is the hottest time of the day. He also notes another unusual feature of the story in that she does this chore alone, rather than with other women, which would have been common during that time: "Both of these things suggest the woman felt a sense of shame and was avoiding contact with other women."[198]

Adding to the odd circumstances of this encounter, it was unusual for men and women who were not family members to talk and interact in this culture. This was made even more notable because Jesus was Jewish and the woman was Samaritan. John writes that, in response to this highly unusual request, the Samaritan woman says to Jesus, "'You are a Jew and I am a Samaritan woman. How can you ask me for a drink?' (For Jews do not associate with Samaritans)" (v. 9). Jesus, however, ignores her brief protest over His socially unacceptable behavior and begins to teach her about living water. He also reveals to her that He knows about her painful past with multiple men (vv. 16-19). He doesn't do this to shame her or cause her guilt. Instead, He reveals His knowledge about her history to increase "her thirst for a meaningful relationship with God."[199]

As this story illustrates, divine encounters can happen to those whom society has rejected, to those who have had difficult lives, to those who live in guilt and shame, and those who are simply going about daily life. And as the Samaritan woman shows, we simply need to stop and lean in when they happen.

Another example of an everyday kind of encounter occurs with two sets of brothers, Simon Peter and Andrew, and James and John (Matt 4:18-22). David Brown notes the lack of fanfare when Jesus finds the brothers at the Sea of Galilee: "Our Lord had made no public appearance in Galilee, and so had gathered none around Him; He is walking solitarily by the shores of the lake when He accosts the two pairs of fishermen."[200] They were preparing their nets, a routine chore performed hundreds of times in their work as fishermen. This time, however, Jesus shows up and changes the mundane to the amazing: "Jesus called them, and immediately they left the boat … and followed him" (Matt 4:21–22). As this story also shows, God breaks through ordinary events. Divine encounters can happen anywhere and to anyone.

Divine Conversion

Paul's life changed significantly after his encounter with Jesus bringing countless people to Christ, and today, similar examples exist of dramatic encounters that lead to unexpected conversions of people who then bring others to Christ. Such is the case of Husein, who had moved from the Middle East to the United States to convert Christians to Islam. One day, during the week of Easter, Husein was watching television when a preacher came on and shared a message. Husein explains what happened next: "Suddenly, the Holy Ghost fell on me! I looked up, and Jesus was there in front of me. I'd been a devout Muslim, but as soon as I saw Him, it was like seeing an old friend I knew before. And I knew it was Jesus. And I knew something else. I knew that He was the Son of God!"[201] Tom Doyle, president and founder of Uncharted Ministries, reports the result of the amazing encounter: "Husein is broadcasting today on television and online into the Middle East, sharing Bible studies and relevant topics with Muslims. He answers questions, prays with people, and leads Muslims to faith in Christ."[202] Husein had a life-changing encounter with Jesus and is a witness to Him amid threats, intimidation, and persecution. He stands strong in his newfound salvation.

Likewise, Noor, a Muslim mother of eight, had a powerful encounter with Jesus, but her encounter happened in a dream. Kamal Assam, a devoted Christian woman living in Cairo, Egypt, listened to Noor's testimony: "Jesus walked with me alongside a lake, and He told me how much He loves me. … All He said was, 'I love you, Noor. I have given everything for you. I died for you.'"[203] For more than three hours, Kamal sat with Noor, answering every question she had about Jesus, teaching her Scripture, and explaining the cost of following Him. Kamal and others, according to Doyle, are considered "the new Josephs, placed there by God to interpret dreams. The need for explanation is so great, in fact, that Uncharted Ministries placed this ad in the *Cairo Times*: 'Have you seen a man in a white robe in a dream? If so, call this number….'"[204] Both of these testimonies describe seeing, changing, and being set on a new course. A changed perspective on God, a new life purpose, and missional obedience followed their encounters with Jesus. Encounters with God, no matter how great or how small, should lead to noticeable changes in us, our message, and our methods.

Experiencing God the Way He Designed Us

Although one might assume that dramatic encounters are the most meaningful or most valid God-encounters, Scripture shows us otherwise. Gary Thomas explains that we each possess natural tendencies to encounter and commune with God. He explores nine different temperaments or pathways in which we can experience God. For each one listed, we will explore an example that, while not earth-shattering, is a valid way to connect with and encounter God.

I'm sure by now you have guessed that my way to connect to God is through creativity. I regularly meet with God in meaningful ways while painting, collaging, and doodling. My encounters with God happen when I do art, which is part of my sensate temperament, according to Thomas. The nine temperaments or pathways to experience God include the following: "Naturalist: Let me be outdoors. Sensate: Let me experience. Traditionalist: Let me remember. Ascetic: Let me be alone. Activist: Let me conquer. Caregiver: Let me care. Enthusiast: Let me celebrate. Contemplative: Let me feel. Intellectual: Let me think."[205]

Naturalists are motivated by a connection to the outdoors. They enjoy outdoor adventures, including connecting with God in settings filled with sun, sky, mountains, streams, and other places without walls. For naturalists, being outside is a sanctuary where they can feel God in nature. Beautiful examples in Scripture of the naturalist pathway are found in the Psalms, which are filled with testimonies to the beauty of the sky, birds, and mountains. The Psalmist compares God's care for humanity by using outdoor examples, such as in Psalm 23.

The sensate pathway describes those who experience God with their senses. As a creative person, I identify as a sensate, but as we briefly touched on in Chapter 3, kinesthetic learners may also identify as sensate. The five senses, which include taste, touch, sight, smell, and sound, are a primary pathway for many to experience God. Ezekiel 1:4 reveals the importance of senses in Scripture: "I looked, and I saw … an immense cloud with flashing lightning and surrounded by brilliant light. The center of the fire looked like glowing metal, and in the fire was what looked like four living creatures." Ezekiel later refers to the sense of taste in his encounter with God: "Then he said to me, 'Son of man, eat this scroll … .' So, I ate it, and it tasted as sweet as honey in my mouth"

(3:3). For sensates, God is encountered through colors, sounds, tastes, fragrances, and textures. These experiences teach them about God, "facilitate dialogue with God, make visible something invisible, and predispose [them] to prayer and contemplation."[206] They can include those who cook and bake, creative people making art, architects inventing structures, singers and musicians, perfumers developing aromas, as well as anyone else who creates, designs, builds, or connects with God as they engage with their senses.

Those who encounter God through tradition value symbols, icons, practices, and rituals. They connect to God through memories, traditions, and remembrances. Traditions also feature prominently in Scripture. In Deuteronomy 6:6-9, for example, God instructs the Israelites to keep His Word bound to their hands and on their foreheads because He wanted them to remember Him by meditating on Scripture. Several times, God instructs the Israelites to erect altars to mark memorable encounters with Him (Exod 20:24-26; 27:1-8; 30:1-10; Deut 27:1-8; Josh 8:30). Sacrifices were also offered to honor God, and symbols were used to proclaim truth about Him. Today, we value the bread and wine or juice that we take for communion in remembrance of Jesus's life and sacrifice.[207]

Ascetics are those who commune with God by strictly following guidelines, live simply, and make significant personal sacrifices. This spiritual temperament is also known as desert spirituality due to the Early Church history of men and women living in the extreme desert environment for personal and spiritual growth. Abba Arsenius, a fourth century desert spiritual father, explained the ascetic way of life to a young disciple: "Strive with all your might to bring your interior activity into accord with God, and you will overcome exterior passions."[208] Ascetics seek to tame the human flesh and worldly desires. Some may interpret ascetics as being legalistic, and, as Thomas points out, "in some cases, it can be. For healthy ascetics, however, strictness is a cherished method of expressing love for God."[209] They emphasize the spiritual development of their inner lives. Notably, while "true ascetics are strict with themselves," they "treat others with supernatural gentleness."[210] They typically enjoy solitude as well and find hard work to be an honoring connection with God. Their commitment, consistency, and discipline are evident in the way they live.

Activists use social action and righteous confrontations to glorify God as they stand for justice. It's easy to recognize Christian activists in history, such as Martin Luther King Jr., Corrie ten Boom, Harriet Tubman, Florence Nightingale, Dietrich Bonhoeffer, and Sojourner Truth, among others. Activists act out of love for God and people, but the activist temperament can be confrontational and sometimes make others feel uncomfortable. This temperament stands against social ills and unrighteous culture—they desire change. Thomas characterizes the activist pathway this way: "While the rest of us prefer to play it safe, activists often exhibit an almost insatiable need to see God break through in mighty ways."[211] Moses, Elijah, Habakkuk, and Peter are some biblical examples of activists standing against injustice with a posture of righteous confrontation.

Those with the caregiver temperament feel closest to God when addressing the real needs of others. The imagery of shepherds caring for sheep in Scripture is an example of caregiving. Jesus describes himself as the Good Shepherd who "lays down his life for his sheep" (John 10:11). His numerous acts of servanthood recorded in the Gospels also demonstrate caregiving as He healed the sick, fed the crowds, and showed profound compassion to people in need (Matt 4:23–24; 6:2; 9:35–36).[212] The theme of caregiving is emphasized all throughout both the Old and New Testaments. Deuteronomy 10:18-19, for example, says, "He defends the cause of the fatherless and the widow, and loves the foreigner residing among you, giving them food and clothing. And you are to love those who are foreigners, for you yourselves were foreigners in Egypt." And the Book of James teaches that faith is expressed through actions toward others: "Suppose a brother or a sister is without clothes and daily food. If one of you says to them, 'Go in peace; keep warm and well fed,' but does nothing about their physical needs, what good is it? In the same way, faith by itself, if it is not accompanied by action, is dead" (Jas 2:15-17). While we all have the mandate to care for others, those with the caregiving temperament especially feel the presence of God as they care for people in need.

Enthusiasts, and Pentecostals in particular, love a good celebration. Their worship is relational, participatory, and grateful. As Jacqueline Grey notes, "There is a conviction that God is truly present in our corporate worship and continues to reveal himself. The sense of immediacy of God's presence is both sought and anticipated in the public worship."[213] They recognize the active presence of God and the Holy Spirit in their lives, and they embrace mysterious and supernatural experiences. They enjoy celebratory acts and jubilant worship as they revel in the excitement of God. They enthusiastically look for spiritual events in their everyday life and embody the worship described in the Book of Psalms: "Shout for joy to the Lord, all the earth. Worship the Lord with gladness; come before him with joyful songs" (Ps 100:1-2). They expect God to move, and they celebrate Him through work, journaling their dreams, exploring creativity, connecting with community, and sharing their triumphant message with others.

Contemplatives, meanwhile, long to spend quiet time in the presence of God. Their adoration and desire to sit at the feet of Jesus is the mark of this temperament. Mary is a prime example of a contemplative. She sat at the feet of Jesus, seeking to learn from Him (Luke 10:38-42).[214] They connect to God as they spend time loving Him, adoring Him, and sitting quietly and in solitude in His presence. John Coe describes the prayer of contemplatives as the kind of prayer that the Apostle Paul models in Ephesians 3:14-19. He describes it as "the act and experience whereby our human spirit opens to and attends to the Indwelling Spirit of Christ, who is continually revealing himself to us."[215] Church history has numerous examples of famous contemplatives, including the Desert Fathers and Mothers, St. Teresa of Avila, and St. John of the Cross. Contemplatives encounter God in reflective, devoted moments, known by their great desire to be nearer to God.

The intellectual pathway regards book learning, reading, and contemplating difficult passages of the Bible as times to honor and encounter God. They connect with God through Bible studies, studying Christian doctrine, thinking through ethical issues, and learning how to defend their faith in God. The Bible emphasizes the need for wisdom, and it honors Solomon for his great wisdom and intellect:

> God gave Solomon wisdom and very great insight, and a breadth of understanding as measureless as the sand on the seashore. … He spoke three thousand proverbs and his songs numbered a thousand and five. He spoke about plant life, from the cedar of Lebanon to the hyssop that grows out of walls. He also spoke about animals and birds, reptiles and fish. From all nations people came to listen to Solomon's wisdom…. (1 Kgs 4:29-34).

A trained mind is a gift to the church. Thomas notes that intellectual pursuits "have played a key role in the advance of God's work" and attributes the success of the Early Church and the spread of the gospel in the world to Christians who were able to "outthink" the pagan world around it.[216] Effective sermons, Bible studies, and discipleship programs require Christians who love to study and teach. As Thomas rightly states, "Any form of Christianity that rejects or even diminishes the importance of the mind is not a biblical Christianity."[217]

No matter what combination of spiritual temperaments we may have, God wants to have interaction and encounter His creation. Gary Tyra reminds us that God the Father is desirous to grow nearer to those who claim to belong to Him:

> Because of the incarnation of Christ and the outpouring of the Holy Spirit on the Day of Pentecost, it is possible for God's human image bearers to really know and experience their creator in some real, phenomenal, life-story shaping way. In other words, their spirituality is not only an acknowledgement of God; it involves the cultivation of a person, intimate, interactive existentially impactful relationship with him as their heavenly Father.[218]

Oftentimes, our flesh desires a quick fix, an event to get us going, yet those events may not provide a means for lasting relationship. This is where cultivating spiritual disciplines enter the picture. Tyra discusses the distinction between occasional and perpetual Christian spirituality with the goal of possessing characteristics like Jesus.[219] An episodic relationship often involves surface-level love while lacking commitment. Chronic spirituality and communion with God constitute a deeper way of life. The perpetual lifestyle is one of daily faithfulness, cultivating a relationship with the Trinity, making space for the Holy Spirit, and spending time in the Word. Spiritual disciplines contribute consistency for the believer's life and support a lifestyle of ongoing spiritual formation.

Richard Foster explains that the value of spiritual disciplines lies in their leading us to God: "The disciplines in themselves are of no value whatsoever. They have value only as a means of setting us before God so that He can give us the liberation we seek. The liberation is the end; the disciplines are merely the means. They are not the answer; they only lead us to the Answer."[220] Additionally, David Setran remarks that "the disciplines allow us to place ourselves before God so that He can transform us. ... They can get us to the place where something can be done. They are God's means of grace."[221]

We can cultivate spiritual encounters with God through the spiritual disciplines, which fall into three categories: 1) the inward disciplines of meditation, prayer, fasting, and study; 2) the outward disciplines of simplicity, solitude, submission, and service; and 3) the corporate disciplines of confession, worship, guidance, and celebration.[222] Additionally, Dallas Willard points out the power of spiritual disciplines to deliver us from the grip of sin. Willard encourages the practical spiritual disciplines of "Bible reading, meditating on Scripture, Scripture memorization, prayer, worship, evangelism, service, stewardship, fasting, silence, solitude, journaling, submission and frugality."[223]

We can encounter God on a regular basis by developing a Rule of Life, a personal framework of spiritual disciplines that we can practice daily, weekly, monthly, annually, and seasonally. Simon Chan asserts that a good Rule of Life will "ensure constancy, regularity and proficiency" as we commit ourselves to a daily rhythm and relationship with God.[224] Some examples of a Rule of Life include the Rule of St. Basil, which includes a commitment to community life, simplicity, prayer, and care for the poor, and the Rule of Benedict, which is a "rhythmic cycle of common prayer, daily work and study."[225]

Other examples may include daily recitations of the Lord's Prayer, the Ten Commandments, a favorite psalm, or another anchoring Scripture passage.[226] Practicing the Rule of Life is a consistent, daily, individualized rhythm for life. In time, this becomes a natural, integrated way to apply various spiritual disciplines.

Creative Encounter

The image of encounter may or may not include a dramatic meeting, such as Saul's. Instead, it might look like a conversation with God during a chore. Think of a time when you encountered the Lord—was it gentle and tender or rather sudden and stern? Use carving or wood-burning tools with a wooden plank or cutting board for this project. Using the word "encounter," mark your wooden piece to represent your encounter with God. Deep marks denote strength and solemnity; light marks denote gentle persuasiveness. If wood tools are unavailable, use paint to write "encounter," and select colors that convey the character or intensity of the meeting.

Remember, too, that art can be a playful endeavor. While the importance of play is recognized in childhood as a fundamental process of learning, it becomes less emphasized as we age. Creativity, as a form of play, is essential to a holistic life. Too often, we are pressured to be serious, stifling our child-like curiosity and playful nature. However, if believers are settled in the arms of God, with His peace surrounding them, why can't we stop striving for a bit and play as we delight in the creativity that flows from God? Of course, we cannot throw away all our obligations and responsibilities for  unending playtime, but could we not use a bit of free play and creativity for a renewing encounter with God?

Application

How has encountering Jesus changed your countenance, perspective, and behavior? How have your spiritual temperaments also influenced your encounters? What spiritual disciplines are the Holy Spirit encouraging you to nurture? Notice the illumination and the change as a result of an encounter with God in your life. In what areas of your life do you need a divine encounter with Jesus for lasting change? Have our encounters with God revealed and illuminated Jesus so we see Him in greater fullness? Have our encounters with God brought about life change and inspired obedient submission? We must make space to encounter God and expect glorious results. A prayer for us as we seek Him: *Lord, illuminate, bring change, and call us to obedience through an encounter with You. Heal all the broken places in our souls so that we can be reflections of You.*

CHAPTER 9: IMAGE OF FEAST

Introduction

In this chapter, we will study the kingdom of God as represented by the image of a feast. The Parable of the Great Banquet in Luke 14:15-24 symbolizes the future heavenly Kingdom and the invitation extended to all humankind to join God. The image of a feast draws our attention to heaven with eternity in view. The theme of feast also appears again one chapter later in the Parable of the Lost Son (15:11-24), in which God invites us to forgiveness to enjoy an amazing, holistic, restored relationship with the Father, and Jesus looks forward to drinking the fruit of the vine with His followers in the Father's Kingdom (Matt 26:29). As we will see, abundance, invitation, and celebration in community make up the image of a feast.

An Invitation to Feast

In the Parable of the Great Banquet, Jesus reveals how the host desires for his house to be full of guests (Luke 14:15-24) to enjoy the "elaborate dinner celebration."[227] All the preparations had been made, and the host sent invitations to the invited guests. However, those who were invited either did not want to go or were uninterested in going, so they devised various reasons for why they would not attend (vv. 18-20). When the host hears their excuses, he becomes angry and tells his servant to find whoever he can, "the poor, the crippled, the blind and the lame" (v. 21). Even after his servant does this, however, there was still more room, so the host instructs his servant to "go out to the roads and country lanes and compel them to come in, so that my house will be full" (v. 23).

Amanda Brobst-Renaud beautifully expresses the great banquet of Luke 14 and describes how the host, despite being let down for non-attendance by his original invitees, radically "reimagines his dinner companions and invites the poor, the crippled, the blind, and the lame. The banquet thrower envisions a future that seems unthinkable—an elite dinner party filled with the socially outcast."[228] Brobst-Renaud illustrates the scene with the newly invited guests: "It is a feast full of people who do not know the rules, who fill the banquet hall with their cacophonous joy at the surprise of the invitation."[229] These individuals would not refuse such a generous invitation to enjoy the festivities and food.

The great banquet reveals the mission of God for all to know Him, as evidenced in the welcome of the unintended guests:

> The church is an inconvenient banquet with a rowdy bunch of attendees, many of whom do not get along, and most of whom are more concerned with where they will sit than with whether there is a seat for their neighbor. Yet the feast is prepared, and the banquet thrower issues the invitation to imagine a different future. In this future, all are welcome because the banquet thrower has declared it to be so. The Great Banquet brings with it the invitation and the promise to satisfy the great hunger of its guests.

Welcome to the feast.[230]

The church can do much more to partner with the Great Host and invite others into the greatest party ever imagined. We can create a space where all are welcomed and celebrated.

Warren W. Wiersbe points to the parable's plea to share the gospel of Jesus Christ to the lost world: "God still says, 'All things are now ready. Come!' Nothing more need be done for the salvation of your soul, for Jesus Christ finished the work of redemption when He died for you on the cross and arose from the dead. The feast has been spread, the invitation is free, and you are invited to come."[231] This welcoming invitation of the feast appears again in the Parable of the Lost Son (Luke 15:11-32). The celebration of the return of the wayward son and the lavish joy the father expresses result in a feast of abundance. The father rejoices at the son's return and receives him not as a servant but as a celebrated son.

Abundance is seen in the forgiveness shown and the father giving the son the best robe, a ring, and sandals. Walter Wiersbe explains the meaning of each of these gifts:

The ring was a sign of sonship, and the "best robe" (no doubt the father's) was proof of his acceptance back into the family (see Gen. 41:42; Isa. 61:10; 2 Cor. 5:21). Servants did not wear rings, shoes, or expensive garments. The feast was the father's way of showing his joy and sharing it with others. Had the boy been dealt with according to the Law, there would have been a funeral, not a feast.[232]

Not only is abundance a theme of this feast, but so is reconciliation, according to Godwin A. Etukumana, who adds that "the father waives the right to employ his paternal power and authority and chooses, in its place, not only to be generous but to be generous to a fault, where mercy mingled with compassion is evidence of abundant grace, a grace that is always unmerited and undeserving."[233] The father shows his abundant grace and generosity to the son as he reconciles with him for all the community to witness.

When imagining the feast thrown by the father for his newly returned son, one cannot help but think of a grand party. Anthony Campolo notes that Jesus loved a good party: "Jesus performed his first miracle at a wedding reception (John 2:1–11). When it looked like the host was running out of wine, Jesus turned some water into wine, just to keep the party going."[234] Campolo also notes that in Deuteronomy 14, when instructions are given about tithing 10 percent, the Law dictates that the collected tithes were to be used for celebration: "Exchange your tithe for silver, and take the silver with you and go to the place the Lord your God will choose. Use the silver to buy whatever you like: cattle, sheep, wine or other fermented drink, or anything you wish. Then you and your household shall eat there in the presence of the Lord your God and rejoice" (vv. 25-26). The feasting presented here is a foretaste of being with God in heaven eternally. In his theology of party, Campolo ecstatically portrays heaven: "The gospel is the good news about the celebration and partying that mark the Kingdom of God, and in the lives of Christians that celebration and partying should already be evident."[235] The image of a feast is joyful, celebratory, and life-giving. It is an invitation to community.

Invitation to Community

Some of us may identify with the wayward son through a community who has witnessed the joy of our recovery and celebrated with us. Having a strong community of support is key to long-term sobriety. Walter Elwell and Philip Comfort note the importance of communal celebration: "When there is communal participation, a festival can reinforce the individual and community memory of specific occasions and can perpetuate that store of recollection over years and generations."[236] It remains important to let others around us rejoice with us as we celebrate sobriety and addiction-free milestones. Celebration with our community is only one of several ways to strengthen our spiritual muscles, and it reflects the biblical concept of koinonia or "fellowship."[237]

Agus Setiawan et al. explains that community support is critical for successful recovery: "Participation in support groups and the establishment of non–addictive social ties can reduce feelings of isolation, strengthen resistance to relapse, and encourage the adoption of healthier behavior patterns."[238] The research emphasizes that social support plays a large role in recovery through healthy connections with family, friends, and networking in the community. Social support encourages accountability, positive synergy for a recovery mindset, and adds tools to the recovery toolbelt.

Not surprisingly, community and fellowship, especially for younger people, have been shown to be highly valuable in drug recovery efforts, while social isolation makes recovery more difficult.[239] A study of 195 youth recovering from addiction over a twelve-month period "found increased risk of relapse, incarceration, and violent crime associated with social isolation," but those who were actively involved in a recovery community "during treatment decreased the likelihood of these outcomes in the year post-treatment. Our results suggest the importance of addressing social isolation by engaging adolescents in social support resources in ways that allow youths to be supported by and contribute to a sober community that extends beyond the treatment period."[240] The study's findings show that community enhances sobriety.

Other studies also reinforce the importance of community support services and participation for sobriety. However, it should be noted that substance abuse is often treated as a short-term medical intervention with the expectation of a full recovery, but, as Rosemary Boisvert et al. observe, "it is unrealistic to expect patients with chronic substance abuse disorder to achieve recovery following a brief intervention."[241] Those who only receive brief intervention experience high rates of relapse, but those who receive community support have significantly better outcomes over the long-term.[242]

In addition, as another study shows, participation in a community support group for recovery has benefits not only for participants but also for those providing the support as peers in recovery:

> While none of the peers interviewed expected to benefit from helping, all reported this experience

to be not only meaningful but also to have a positive impact on their recovery. Providing peer support to others strengthened the workers' ability to maintain personal recovery by keeping them connected to communities of support, providing opportunities to be of service, allowing them to pay forward what had been given to them, and a sense of accomplishment in being a part of the recovery of another individual. This study highlighted that helping others is a benefit to both the recovery of peer support workers and their personal lives, while recognizing the need to separate personal recovery efforts from helping.[243]

It appears that community, or koinonia, is a life-giving principle for all involved, whether those new to their journey of recovery or those sharing the wisdom of their recovery, just as the Apostle Paul taught.

The most effective forms of community for long-term recovery are residential and faith-based. Aaron Todd Bicknese has done extensive research on the effectiveness of the Teen Challenge program in comparison to non-faith-based treatment programs, such as short-term inpatient programs (STI) and STI coupled with participation in Alcoholics Anonymous. The findings of his research demonstrate that long-term, faith-based residential programs have significantly higher rates of success "on the outcomes of employment, addictive substance usage, severity of relapse, and severity of depression," underscoring the importance of making Jesus the Lord of one's life and the benefits of a strong, ongoing Christian support community for sobriety.[244] Particularly effective is long-term residential 24-hour support for overall spiritual health.

The late David Wilkerson, who founded Teen Challenge in 1958 as part of his lifelong ministry of working with youth struggling with addiction and crime, identified loneliness as the primary driver of addiction. As Bicknese explains,

> The central issue for [Wilkerson] remains that of loneliness, which often prompts a shell of pride, arrogance, or complacency "to hide the real, scared, lonely" individual. Drug abuse, then, is but a symptom of the deeper problem, loneliness, which can only be addressed adequately at the spiritual level by a personal relationship with God, and at the social level by a close-knit Christian community for material and morale-building needs which the new believer

may face.[245]

Living in a Christian community not only encourages accountability for behavior, but it also addresses the root problem of acceptance and loneliness, as shown by the testimony of an Adult and Teen Challenge graduate, who describes how prior to their participation in this community, "I thought no one could ever understand and bring me out of the endless suffering I was in. At Teen Challenge, God showed me His amazing grace and opened up my heart to let others in to help. I now know it is not all about me but about helping others and showing love, forgiveness and accepting others for who they are."[246]Communal living is a lifestyle centered around sharing living spaces and resources with others in the community. This way of life fosters a sense of togetherness and encourages individuals to develop selflessness and compassion when interacting with others.

Living in a communal setting means people are responsible for their own and the community's well-being. This model of community living protects against selfishness, which is a common issue in addiction recovery. Communal living involves sharing household chores, cooking meals together, and helping to maintain the living space. By embracing a spirit of selflessness and compassion, individuals in communal living can build stronger relationships and develop a deeper sense of community among one another. This fosters a positive and constructive environment and creates a support system that can help individuals through tough times. Overall, communal living is a unique lifestyle that offers many benefits for those willing to embrace it.

By prioritizing the community's well-being, individuals can find greater purpose and fulfillment in their daily lives. Community living can also help individuals develop healthy physical habits that replace harmful and toxic ones, improving overall well-being and longevity. Communities that also provide physical exercise and nutrition counseling services provide a more holistic approach for residents' recovery, as these two areas significantly affect physical health and overall well-being. Furthermore, they can cultivate life skills that promote holistic rejuvenation of the soul, mind, and emotions, which also profoundly impact one's physical health and vitality.

The value of being in community is hard to overstate. Irwyn Ince notes that a thriving community reflects the image of God. Ince reminds those who have struggled with addiction that our challenges bring our story to life: "God is the one who writes our life's story of faith in Jesus Christ. It is often the case that His Spirit uses this story to ignite a ministry passion in us. People who God delivers from addiction become passionate about seeing and helping others know that same deliverance."[247] I wholeheartedly agree with Ince, and I would add that by sharing our story of addiction and triumph with others in community gives us a platform from which to proclaim truth once we have overcome and been delivered.

We are not meant to live in isolation. We have community and God with us, and the image of feast represents this. The father in the parable had more than enough to share and celebrate with the community, as he declared, "Bring the fattened calf and kill it. Let's have a feast and celebrate. For this son of mine was dead and is alive again; he was lost and is found.' So they began to celebrate" (Luke 15:23–24). Like the father and son in this parable, we express gratitude in community when we celebrate with each other because our Father in heaven also has more than enough for us.

Creative Encounter

The image of feasting can be expressed in many ways. Focus on abundance, celebration, or communion.

At what times were you especially close to the Father? Do you have one area of abundance in your life? Think about abundance and create a canvas with Scriptures from an abandoned hymnal. Find Scriptures that speak of His nearness to you or the joyful freedom you have. Use Mod Podge to adhere the verses and music lyrics to the canvas.

Another option is to take a canvas and paint your name in the middle. Express the celebration that God has for you with glitter sparkles, sprays of color, and confetti. Does the story of the Father running to his son resonate with you? What robe did He cover you with? What ring did He put on your finger, and what sandals are on your feet?

Another idea is to design and create an invitation to come to the marriage supper of the Lamb. Make it elaborate, with beautiful script and maybe pearls and gold lettering. Add your name to the front and sign it from the host, God. How can you express the image of feasting? Looking closer at the image of the feast. What is one aspect of feasting that makes your heart desire more of God?

Application

Have you been received as a wayward son? Or are you still waiting for your family to reconcile with you? The unfortunate reality is that years of reckless living bring pain and consequences. The separation of our loved ones causes us to look forward even more to the kingdom of God, when the complete restoration of all things is achieved. Until then, here are some ways to keep your mind on God as you wait: Get involved in your community. Build camaraderie with fellow workers. Take part in the Lord's Supper with your community of faith and unite with a healthy family when possible.

Community involvement can take place in your local town, such as serving in a volunteer position, offering to sit with a senior citizen, pet sitting, or serving on a town board. Nonprofits are always seeking volunteers for front-office work, groundskeeping, or fundraising events. Being part of your local town or city is a wonderful way to reach out beyond yourself. Seeing the needs around you helps to keep your mind on the Lord.

Since work takes up a large portion of our waking hours, we should be aware of the type of work crews and co-workers we spend time with. We may need to practice patience when working with those who are not in recovery or are not sensitive to recovery values. Work gives us an opportunity to share testimonies of the goodness and salvation of Jesus.

Most places of worship have a regular time for communion, also known as the Lord's Supper. This important act is done with the faith community to remember the Lord Jesus until He comes again. Receiving communion in your community fosters a sense of spiritual closeness among one another. The intimacy of communion, which focuses on repentance and on Jesus, is a beautiful declaration to make together, as we look forward to celebrating with Jesus, who says, "Take and eat; this is my body. … Drink from it, all of you. This is my blood of the covenant, which is poured out for many for the forgiveness of sins. I tell you, I will not drink from this fruit of the vine from now on until that day when I drink it new with you in my Father's kingdom" (Matt 26:26-29). What a glorious celebration we will have in heaven! Until then, we can rejoice and remember the Lord Jesus as a community. The Lord's Supper is a sign of unity among the community who share in the body and blood of Jesus. It also proclaims the Cross as we await Christ's return.

Spending time with a healthy family can be challenging because of past relationships. Often, the family holds onto unforgiveness and resentment. Some families are neither safe nor beneficial. We cannot be expected to navigate others' emotions. We can, however, walk in our newfound freedom and healing with confidence that Christ has reconciled us to himself. This reconciliation brings joy and the abundant life that others will notice. We can be patient with our family who have not embraced freedom. Be intentional about positioning yourself around healthy family members. Limit exposure to unhealthy people, which is critical for maintaining a recovery mindset.

CHAPTER 10: IMAGE OF WORK

Introduction

Work is both what we do through "labor, skill, and time" in exchange for "monetary and intrinsic rewards" as well as "an exercise of stewardship."[248] The mandate to work and labor was not a curse given by God. Instead, God created work and the stewardship of our resources as part of His creation. It was His way of loving Adam and Eve, the created animals, and the Garden. Our dignity is tied to work, and it takes effort to work, labor, toil, be employed, and do all the activities needed to sustain life. The image of work has implications for the economy, our morals, and our spirituality. Scripture portrays work through the stories of the potter, mason, tentmaker, mother, father, wife, husband, herdsman, shepherd, farmer, ironsmith, carpenter, merchant, fisherman, and artist, among others.

Scripture consistently refers to the mandate to work when one has the ability and capacity to work. The first reference occurs in the beginning, when God gives Adam and Eve dominion over the earth and its creatures (Gen 1:28). He also directs Adam to work the garden (2:15). Later, when giving the Israelites the Law, God commands, "Six days you shall labor and do all your work, but the seventh day is a sabbath to the Lord your God. On it you shall not do any work…." (Exod 20:9-10). Work is also discussed in the Gospels and then by Apostle Paul, who reminds disruptive troublemakers that "the one who is unwilling to work shall not eat" (2 Thess 3:10). Even when God establishes the new heaven and the new earth, Isaiah prophesies that people "will build houses and dwell in them; they will plant vineyards and eat their fruit. No longer will they build houses and others live in them, or plant and others eat. … My chosen ones will long enjoy the work of their hands" (Isa 65:21-22). Not only do we work, but God himself also works, as shown by His creation of the universe, the earth, and humankind, as well as His ongoing work in our daily lives.[249]

Examples of Workers in Scripture

Lydia

The New Testament tells of those who used their day job as mission work. Paul, Priscilla, and Aquila, for example, were tentmakers (Acts 18:3), while Lydia was a businesswoman, a household overseer, and supporter of her community's economy (Acts 16). Acts narrates how Paul and his companions go outside the city gate and down to a river as they look for a place to pray. There they find Lydia and a group of women and begin to teach them. After receiving Paul's message, Lydia and her household are baptized, and she persuades Paul and his companions to stay at her house (vv. 13–15).

The Theology of Work Project highlights the unique role that Lydia played in building the church when she invites them to stay at her house:

> There in her large house she began the first Christian church on Greek soil, welcoming other new believers into the fellowship of faith. Lydia was successful both in her professional work

and in her social or spiritual work nurturing the nascent Greek church. Most likely the knowledge and connections she cultivated as a trader helped her in her church work, and vice versa. In Lydia we see a woman whose skill and interest is not confined to one limited area. Indeed, we see that both her position in commerce and her knowledge of faith made her uniquely qualified to spearhead the church in Greece.[250]

Indeed, as a merchant of purple cloth, Lydia would have been quite industrious and wealthy. She ran a household and was equipped to offer Jewish hospitality and accommodations for the travelers in her home. The dye used to make the purple cloth for Lydia's business, according to Craig Keener, was created by grinding shellfish from Tyre or the lesser-costing madder plant: "Some estimate that it took 10,000 shellfish to produce a little of the costly dye; despite the foul odor associated with the dye, its rareness made it a symbol of wealth and power."[251] Lydia, as an entrepreneur, used her work as an opportunity to serve God.

Prior to her encounter with Paul, Scripture describes Lydia as a "worshiper of God" (Acts 16:14). Christopher Wright points out that after her and the other women's conversions, Paul does not ask the converts to leave their occupations and start preaching: "On the contrary, Paul seems to envisage most of them still there, working and earning, paying their taxes, and doing good in the community. One imagines the Philippian jailer back at his post, Lydia carrying on her textile business, and Erastus somehow combining his ministry as 'mayor of Corinth' with helping Paul's ministry too."[252] The new believers were already stationed and ready to make a difference in their local markets, public places, and workstations.

Jesus

Jesus of Nazareth was also no stranger to work. The Gospel of Mark describes Him as a "carpenter" (6:3), which likely indicates that Jesus was either a builder or craftsman. When Jesus spent the last three years of His life preaching the gospel and ministering to the people, He often taught using examples, stories, and parables that relied on ordinary work to teach Kingdom truths, work ethics, and stewardship. He taught that neighborly love can be expressed through our work as we allow our faith and work to intersect.

Jesus's teachings spanned a wide variety of work scenarios including agriculture and farming, such as the Parable of the Tenants in Mark 12:1-12; construction and craftsmanship, such as the Wise and Foolish Builders in Luke 6:46-49;

fishing (e.g., Parable of the Net in Matthew 13:47-52), management (e.g., Parable of the Workers in the Vineyard, Matthew 20:1-16), household and service work (e.g., the Watchful Servants in Mark 13:34-27), and shepherding and animal care (e.g., Parable of the Lost Sheep, Luke 15:3-7). Jesus regularly used the imagery of work to convey truth about the dignity of labor, God's idea of generosity and fairness, the moral and spiritual realities of daily life, principles of God's Kingdom, and the need to remain spiritually alert, diligent, and faithful in our endeavors.

In summary, Tom Nelson asserts that work is an act of loving one's neighbors: "What a remarkable testimony to the hard work that neighborly love requires. When people are motivated and able to work, economic flourishing often emerges."[253] Setting our minds on eternal life and engaging in daily life through work is a spiritual discipline that must be intentionally cultivated, according to theologians at Theology of Work:

> When Christians "put to death" (Col. 3:5) the person they used to be, they are then to put on the person God wants them to be, the person God is recreating in the image of Christ (Col. 3:10). This does not consist in hiding oneself away for constant prayer and worship (though

we are all called to pray and worship, and some may be called to do that as a full-time vocation). Rather, it means reflecting God's own virtues of "compassion, kindness, humility, meekness and patience" (Col. 3:12) in whatever we do.[254]

Whether we work at home, work in the marketplace, or give our time and effort to help others, we reflect God's goodness in our homes and in our communities.

David Jones emphasizes that because God works, we, as His image bearers, should also work:

As fallen image-bearers of God, living in a cursed creation, sometimes we will be lazy, and our work will not be as productive as it could otherwise be. At other times we will overwork and idolize wealth. Yet, despite these challenges, the secret to contentment is to faithfully bear the image of God by working, as we look forward to the day when, as Rom. 8:18–21 teaches, both ourselves and the created order will be transformed at Jesus' return.[255]

Until Jesus's return, however, we need to have a healthy view of work, neither being slackers nor working without a regular rhythm of rest. When Jesus returns to set up His Kingdom on earth, labor and jobs will not end. We will all continue to serve one another in love and generosity.

In the meantime, we will continue to fulfill the commandments of God found in Ephesians: "For we are God's handiwork, created in Christ Jesus to do good works, which God prepared in advance for us to do" (2:10). Just as Scripture illustrates with Lydia and Jesus and His teachings, as well as countless others in Scripture, God uses us to steward our surroundings and contribute our talents for the sake of building up others.

The Economy of God

The economy of God includes trusting in God as our provider, alleviating poverty, and assisting our neighbors. This happens through stewardship. As followers of Jesus, our efforts to balance responsibilities and steward well are not ours alone. We have the Holy Spirit to guide us in leading a balanced life and addressing every concern. Believers are "no longer desperately dependent on trying to do the right thing in order to earn God's approval but still committed to try to do the right thing as defined by the character of our Lord and Savior, the carpenter of Nazareth, in whose footsteps we follow as we go about our daily work."[256] Trust in God for our daily needs helps us let go of workaholic tendencies and fosters the faith that He will provide for us.

A critical component of knowing our purpose is appreciating our relationship to work and respecting its significance. We spend a lot of time at our workplaces. The Bureau of Labor Statistics notes that "employed individuals spend approximately 30% to 35% of their waking hours at work."[257] Richard Bliese rightly notes the importance of work in the believer's life: "Work is important to God. Your work is important to God. Your work matters. [This] is how God manages the world. God is loving the world through you and your work."[258]

God used Paul to show His love to the Thessalonians. Paul speaks of his time in ministry there: "Surely you remember, brothers and sisters, our toil and hardship; we worked night and day in order not to be a burden to anyone while we preached the gospel of God to you" (1 Thess 2:9). The word "toil" in this passage implies an "activity that is burdensome" and done as a "labor of love."[259] Indeed, our work is a labor of love for others, and God shows His love for people through our work.

Employment After Addiction

As we either continue working while we recover or need to re-enter the workforce, we need to keep in mind how our workplaces and values interact with sober living. Flourishing in the workplace can be challenging no matter what, but it can be especially difficult for those of us who have overcome addiction. Holding a job after addiction recovery presents challenges, such as missteps or navigating disappointments. These can be prevented by intentionally staying in community with other believers, studying Scripture, reflecting on identity, serving others, and confronting idols. Once we leave the safe and protective confines of rehab, we need to think through our transition back to the workplace, where we learn to maintain sobriety in the "real world." A transformed life can thrive in a marketplace job, but we must be intentional about seeking creative, supportive environments for discipleship and addiction recovery in the workplace. The disciplines learned and healthy habits formed in a recovery program must not be forgotten. Take those workbooks out of storage and keep them before your eyes.

Those in recovery need to work with their supervisors to discuss performance expectations, especially since time management skills may be lacking. Recovering individuals may be struggling with clear thinking, reasoning, and memory, all of which can affect job stability. Additionally, some people experience diminished emotional intelligence. They may have trouble recognizing their own and others' emotions, leading to difficulties in relationships with coworkers. Due to these conditions, it is important to be transparent with colleagues and one's trusted community. Supervisors and coworkers need to understand that the recovery journey can be uneven and sometimes hit plateaus, and a supportive workplace community is crucial for ongoing success and recovery.

When we have our identity secured in Christ, who purchased our redemption with the Father, we are less likely to overwork and strive to prove our worth to others. Instead, work becomes a means for stewarding our lives and our resources and sharing the beauty of God with our families, neighbors, and communities. Recognizing our God-given identity is key to complete healing. As we become new creations in Christ, our identity becomes more apparent.

Work is a sacred activity, whether it occurs within the church, home, or in the marketplace.[260] Still, as Amy Sherman rightly points out, our identity and value do not come from our work:

> What messages does the world feed us about our work? For one, we're inundated with the message that we need to over-work. Americans work more hours than citizens of nearly any other country. I've begun to realize how I've fallen into this trap myself. I've been struggling

with health issues in the past couple of years. This year I'm paring back my work to give myself time to heal and recuperate. I've felt embarrassed because I'm not as busy as I usually am. The fact that I feel embarrassed because I'm not busy enough is a clue to me that work is an idol.[261]

By valuing yourself, you can value and appreciate others and work better with them as God builds teams to advance His name because communities need to see a representation of a Jesus who heals. Colossians 3:23 states, "And whatever you do, do it heartily, as for the Lord and not for men, knowing that from the Lord you will receive the reward of the inheritance."

Creative Encounter

Imagine that you could do anything and make a living at it. When my brother and I were kids, we used to dig tunnels in the hillside and play for hours in the dirt with Hot Wheels. Now he owns and operates an earth excavation company. He drives tractors and earth movers for his living. His play turned into construction dirt work, which provides for his family. When I was young, I wanted to be a roller skate instructor. However, I never did learn to skate backwards, but the idea of it still makes me smile! I still imagine to this day what it would have been like to supervise a skate rink with its perpetual party of people, music, and laughter!

Do you currently work at your dream job? If you could do anything, what would it be? What would you get up early for, and what would you go to bed late for? God has given you unique talents and abilities to enrich your life. Let's capture the image of a work that makes you come alive. Perhaps God will spark a new job venture in your heart.

Make a collage on a canvas board of your dream job. Find some magazines or advertisements of your dream job and choose a few that represent a future hope for work. Add your name and a job title in bold print, such as "Chef Dianne" or "Chris, Lead Tractor Operator," or "Grill Master Colton." Make a collage on your canvas board, envisioning a profitable, mission-as-work dream job. Remember, this is about connecting to God. Nobody will judge your canvas or your dream job. Do not be discouraged if employment opportunities have not come to you. Recall that God is working in the background for your good and His glory.

Application

Work gives us the opportunity to share our witness of Christ, financially give to the mission of God, and edify others. When we view our workplace as a platform for serving others and for serving God, we can keep selfishness and idleness at bay. We can ensure that our work does not become an idol or "disordered love."[262] Serving others shifts the focus away from ourselves and embodies the commandment to love our neighbors. Because those of us with addictions often exhibit selfishness, our affections must be reshaped to prioritize others above ourselves.

Working in service to God and others requires working and living with integrity, according to Wendy Buttacy, who writes, "People of godly integrity become a blessing to everyone they encounter, especially their children. What legacy do you want to build for others? Will your life pass on blessings?"[263] Your testimony is lived out with your good work ethic, integrity and joy. These attributes speak of Christ's reconciliation in our lives, building a better future for our families.

As income starts to flow through your wallet, here are some tips to help you focus on establishing new habits of success: "Sobriety is not an easy feat, and you should be rewarded for your efforts. To stay motivated and on track during drug and alcohol recovery, establish a healthy reward system."[264] This can include regularly adding money to a reward fund, starting a new collection, planning a special trip, or creating other worthwhile, motivating rewards to support daily sober living. These ideas are simple and effective ways to support sobriety.

Whether employed or unemployed, we must be watchful about idleness. Has idleness ever brought you trouble? Paul warns the Thessalonians about busybodies and contrasts laziness with those who faithfully contribute to their livelihoods in 2 Thessalonians 3:6-13. Those recovering from addictions must intentionally avoid idleness and time wasting. Doing godly work can take a variety of forms, such as volunteering, sharing the gospel, mentoring others, counseling, listening, attending training or classes, exercising, and planning meals. These are all examples of fruitful work that guards against idleness.

Our work pleases God as we reflect His name and glory in every aspect of life. The time and energy devoted to family and daily tasks hold great value. Work done at home is no less significant to the Lord. In fact, our first obligation, if we have kids, is to instruct them in the Lord (Deut 11:19). We must be mindful not to diminish the importance of these activities taking place in our homes. The church, as well as the home front, serves as a place to educate people, hear the anointed Word of God, worship together, and serve one another.

Starting a business can be an avenue for serving and nurturing individuals through friendship evangelism, and, in some instances, it can offer a platform for hosting prayer or Bible study groups. The opportunities are endless when one understands that all work is sacred. As Timothy Keller notes, our work is a means by which God loves and cares for His world through us.[265] Work helps us to thrive because we are sharing God's love and care with the world, and our faith, according to Keller, "gives us a new world-and-life view that shapes the character of our work."[266]

Once sobriety and salvation take hold of our lives, it is common to believe that we are being called into professional ministry out of gratitude to God for the changes in our lives. I would like to suggest, however, that full-time ministry is not the only response of gratitude. The world also needs sold-out believers in the workplace, the market, the schools, and the home front. Ministry is a powerful calling for some, but we are all priests and ministers of reconciliation in whatever we do. As the folks at Theology of Work remind us, "A call to ministry or church work is no more sacred than a call to other types of work. What matters most is not one's job title or place of work but obedience to God, the one who calls us. All Christians are called (that is, commanded) to conduct everything they do, round the clock, as full-time service to Christ."[267] This larger calling and the truth that all work is sacred must remain at the forefront of our minds.

Amy Sherman also emphasizes that all work is sacred: "It's imperative that we stop thinking that 'full-time Christian service' is godlier than being a banker, a veterinarian, an engineer, a scientist or a [fill in the blank with your vocation]." When lay workers recognize the goodness of the Lord in their everyday tasks, they will lead fruitful, glory-filled lives. This shift in perspective enables the Spirit to fully manifest on the earth. She adds, "We bloom when we conduct our work in functional, daily reliance on the Spirit, … honor God through our ethical practice, …and relate lovingly with co-workers, as winsome witnesses to the transforming power of a personal relationship with Jesus."[268]

Aside from the spiritual value of work, work also personally benefits us beyond just a paycheck. As Kirsten Nilsson's research shows, it can help us maintain good mental health. Her research on the longevity and health of older employees shows that work satisfaction is connected to employees' motivation level, and the satisfaction of meaningful work is tied to positive mental health: "Individuals who experience a high level of satisfaction in their occupation and perceive their work tasks as very meaningful can, if they are forced to leave their work, often show deteriorated mental health after retirement, unless they have any equally meaningful tasks to engage in as pensioners."[269] Though Nilsson's research focused on the mental health benefits of work among older adults, it is entirely true that work benefits our health regardless of age.

In closing, I can't help but think about Caleb in the Book of Joshua, ready to take on these hills and battle in his advanced years:

> Now then, just as the Lord promised, he has kept me alive for forty-five years.... So here I am today, eighty-five years old! I am still as strong today as the day Moses sent me out; I'm just as vigorous to go out to battle now as I was then. Now give me this hill country that the Lord promised me that day. You yourself heard then that the Anakites were there and their cities were large and fortified, but, the Lord helping me, I will drive them out just as he said (Josh 14:10–12).

Though Caleb was likely considerably older than any of you when he stated this, it is my prayer that we, as recovering addicts, can identify with his "can do" frame of mind that comes from the Lord, regardless of the number of years we have spent in addiction.

CHAPTER 11: IMAGE OF WHOLENESS

Introduction

A holistic approach to formation begins with attending to the human spirit, which includes the intellect, emotions, physical body, vocation, relational aspects, and, of course, cultural dimensions. Cultivating godly virtues, moral excellence, and character shows the world and our family that we desire to live ethically. To flourish in the kingdom of God, we need holistic health, which requires tending and nurturing all aspects of our lives.

Holistic Health

Caring for the Spirit

Scripture describes the human spirit in a variety of ways. It can be provoked or roused (Acts 17:16) or refreshed (2 Cor 7:13), and in Acts 18:25, the trait of a fiery spirit led Apollos to boldly proclaim that Jesus was the Messiah. William Arndt et al. define the human spirit as "the source and seat of insight, feeling, and will, generally as the representative part of human inner life."[270] Other writers assess the human spirit as a "breeze, breath, wind, spirit, sense, mind, intellect frame of mind."[271] Roland Lowther explains that various words in Scripture refer to the human spirit because both Hebrew and Greek lack a dedicated word that only means "spirit."[272]

The human spirit houses the essence of God, and because of this, according to Eugene Carpenter and Philip Comfort, it "corresponds with the nature of God, which is Spirit."[273] Carpenter and Comfort note that scholars are divided over whether the human spirit is "the same as the 'soul."[274] These differences lead to two veins of thought concerning the nature of human beings. Humans are either tripartite, comprising a spirit, soul, and body, or bipartite, consisting of only body and soul. Jan A. Sigvartsen and James H.

Charlesworth express that the bipartite view "suggests a person is both a body and a soul, which lives on after the physical death of a person."[275]

Either way, Jesus clearly calls for the rebirth and renewal of the human spirit as He openly instructs Nicodemus: "Truly, truly, I say to you, unless a man is born of water and the Spirit, he cannot enter the kingdom of God" (John 3:6). In this text, the "Spirit" (πνεῦμαα, τος) refers to the third person of the Trinity. Warren W. Wiersbe points out that "the new birth from above is a necessity..., but it is also a mystery. Everyone who is born of the Spirit is like the wind: you cannot fully explain or predict either the wind or the child of God! For that matter, human birth is still a mystery, in spite of all that we know about anatomy and physiology."[276] Edwin A. Blum agrees, adding that, because we are fallen, we must be born of the Spirit to enter the Kingdom: "A fallen person cannot regenerate himself; he needs a divine operation. Only God's Holy Spirit can regenerate a human spirit. ... They must be born from above. The necessity is absolute and is universally binding."[277]

The Holy Spirit transforms the human spirit and enables it to flourish. The spirit must, therefore, be reborn and restored to fellowship with Christ for eternal life. Walter Elwood and Philip Wesley Comfort beautifully sum up rebirth: "Since the day of regeneration, a believer's human spirit is united to Christ's Spirit."[278] Jesus breathed on the disciples, and they received the Holy Spirit; the inner presence became the revitalizing new life that Jesus gives to those who surrender their lives to Him. A flourishing spirit depends on the vital presence of the Holy Spirit, which is found only through a reborn relationship (John 14:17). Spiritual renewal includes mindful yielding to Christ, dependence upon Him, holy living, and submission to the Holy Spirit.

Praxis for cultivating a healthy spirit begins with rebirth. As Jesus explained to Nicodemus in John 3:6, one must be reborn to understand God's teachings. Meditating on God's Word is an effective way to maintain spiritual well-being. Incorporating Scripture into daily life is essential for building resilience in the face of life's challenges. By hiding the Word of God in one's heart, a person develops a strong foundation, helping them to persevere through tough times. Such practices deeply impact an individual's emotional and spiritual health.

Tending to our spiritual health also involves the practical side of daily abiding in Him. In John 15:5, Jesus calls us to "remain in Me, as I also remain in you. As the branch cannot bear fruit by itself, unless it remains on the vine, neither can you, unless you remain in Me." Abiding includes developing and maintaining a healthy relationship with the

Father, Son, and Holy Spirit. Edward Blum explains how a disciple grows through relationship: "It can mean, first, to accept Jesus as Savior. Second, it can mean to continue or persevere in believing. Third, it can also mean loving obedience (John 15:9–10)."[279] Abiding consists of moments of intimacy, times of grief, or joyous celebration, as well as the mundane things of life and daily interactions with the Trinity.

Soul Care

Holistic health also requires robust soul care. The soul can be afflicted, isolated, and inconsolable. We invest a significant amount of energy in struggles of the soul. Joel Hamme emphasizes that the soul "thinks, feels, acts, and desires."[280] In both the Old Testament and New Testament, the soul (*nepes* and *psyche*) is considered the "inner self, life, and person," the "life force of a person or animal."[281] The soul, then, must be renewed, refreshed, and awakened to its real love, Jesus Christ. All desires must submit to God's Word for soul upkeep. Benjamin Davis explains that the soul needs restoration: "The *nepeš* is revived and refreshed by Yahweh and his law."[282] Psalm 23:3 states, "He restores my soul; He leads me in paths of righteousness for His name's sake." The Psalmist also seeks rescue of his soul from destruction (35:17) because he knows that the Lord is the source of restoration.

Cultivating a healthy soul includes purging selfish wants and desires. As one studies the Bible and gets nearer to Christ, an insightful realization dawns: Idols plague the soul. This insight can serve as a catalyst for personal growth and spiritual awakening. There is no other God besides the one true God of the universe; however, humankind has created its own gods. These gods are worshipped and given authority in addiction, leading to substance abuse. Christopher Wright passionately calls attention to idolatry, rightly stating, "When people worship creation instead of the Creator, everything is turned upside down. Idolatry produces disorder in all our fundamental relationships."[283] The chaos and disorder that follow the person in addiction are evidenced by the trail of broken commitments, broken families, and ruined lives. Jesus, however, establishes His name above the name of ruin and addiction.

When a transformation occurs in the heart, a right relationship with the one and only true God is formed, replacing any idols that previously occupied the heart. This is commonly known as rebirth or salvation. The heart has desires that oppose God's desire for humankind. According to the Bible, believers must humble themselves and engage their will to change. The goal is to participate in the divine nature and become like Christ. Submission to Christ and obeying His direction will bring soul health.

Holiness is achieved through repentance. Ephesians 5:4 clearly states God's expectations of us as a "glorious church, not having spot, or wrinkle, or any such thing, but that it should be holy and without blemish." God desires for us to be holy and pure. God is looking to iron out all the wrinkles in our lives, like the old cast-iron irons that were heated on the stove and then moved back and forth over the cloth until no wrinkle remains. Lots of heat and lots of pressure remove wrinkles.

During one intense season in my life, I desperately desired to see God, but the Spirit impressed upon me that I couldn't see Him until He first showed me something important. I then had a vision of a white paper roll unrolled on the ground like a roll of calculator paper. Documented on the roll were actions and sins that I had committed. Some were forgotten, some were minor, and others were grave sins against God. I didn't want to see my sins spelled out this way, but I needed to admit to them and take ownership. The revelation of the sins was nearly overpowering as I bowed on the ground. I agreed that I had committed each of these, and as I did, the hand of Jesus squeezed a drop of blood on the offense, causing each to vanish as it had never happened. The list seemed to go on and on as I acknowledged and repented, with Jesus forgiving each one. By the time He and I were done, I was in the presence of God. The light was so bright and pure around me. His holiness overwhelmed me. We need to agree with God about our sin. We must inquire, "God, what is your perspective on holiness? My attitude and behavior will change when I get Your perspective. How do I keep from sin?"

Once, when we pastored a youth group, I told the teens I had baked them brownies as a treat. In response to their cheers, I went on to teach about holiness and said that I had added a little bit of puppy poop to the brownie batter. I told them, "But it was a tiny amount, and it was from a very cute puppy!" The youth all booed in response. I told the group that we do the same thing when we keep small amounts of sin and think it doesn't matter. The truth is that our "little" sins aren't cute; our bad habits are really disgusting to God. God is coming for a church without spot or wrinkle; through Jesus's sacrifice, we can be pure. Let's commit to making space to hear what the Spirit wants to reveal in our hearts concerning hidden sins or issues that continually arise. God wants to pull the sin's roots out as if it were a weed. We cannot simply just cut off the top of sin. We have to get rid of the roots for it to be gone forever.

Caring for the Mind

In addition to caring for our soul, holistic health also requires careful attention to the mind, which includes the thoughts and attitudes that significantly influence one's spiritual growth as a Christian. The ancient Greeks believed the mind (νοῦς, διάνοια, φρονέω) was solely responsible for intellect and understanding, and they associated it, according to David Emmanuel, "with understanding, thinking, intelligence, the processing of information, and attitude."[284] The Hebrews, meanwhile, considered the mind interconnected with the soul, spirit, and heart.[285]

One's perception and thoughts about God are critical to cultivating the mind of Christ. A. W. Tozer famously declared that a sanctified mind could prevent sin and temptation: "It is morally imperative that we purge from our minds all ignoble concepts of the Deity and let Him be the God in our minds that He is in His universe."[286] Keeping one's mind and thoughts focused on God's Word is essential for both avoiding sin and fostering spiritual development and growth. Elwell and Comfort explain that transformed believers receive "power to make proper value judgments. Such people have new minds with which to make spiritual discernments."[287] The transformed life and renewed mind give believers discernment because believers possess "the mind of Christ" (1 Cor 2:19).

The Apostle Paul emphasizes the importance of the baptism in the Holy Spirit for a healthy, God-pleasing thought life: "Present your bodies as a living sacrifice, holy, and acceptable to God, which is your reasonable service of worship. Do not be conformed to this world, but be transformed by the renewing of your mind, that you may prove what is the good and acceptable and perfect will of God" (Rom 12:1). Rick Brannan explains that Paul is teaching believers to orient their thinking to cultivate "unity, servanthood, humility, and sacrificial living."[288]

Arndt et al. remark that the sanctified mind is also crucial for mental health well–being: "The key to having a healthy mind lies in selfless and sacrificial living, which was modeled by Jesus. In Matthew 22:37, Jesus said to him, 'You shall love the Lord your God with all your heart, and with all your soul, and with all your mind.' Here, the mind is the faculty of thinking, comprehending, reasoning, understanding, and intelligence."[289] Paul gives instructions for keeping one's mind free from anxiety and chaotic agitation and, instead, to think on "whatever things are true, whatever things are honest, whatever things are just, whatever things are pure, whatever things are lovely, whatever things are of good report if there is any virtue, and if there is any praise...." As one's mind dwells on these things, it reflects healthy behavior and healthy speech. I like to ask, "What does my Father think about X, Y, and Z?" This helps my thinking to line up with what the Father is thinking. It is our responsibility to cultivate a healthy mind. As Dallas Willard writes, we need to "progressively replace our destructive images with the images and ideas that fill the mind of Jesus himself."[290]

The mind focused on God brings honor and glory to Him. Furthermore, as Diane Chandler states, "God has given humans an intellect in which to think, reason, and understand, reflecting God's own nature."[291] Believers replace self-serving views with thoughts and the mind of Christ, "making it obedient to Christ." [292] Paul directs us to demolish thinking that "sets itself up against the knowledge of God" and then "take captive every thought to make it obedient to Christ" (2 Cor 10:5). The act of cultivating obedience can serve as a means of practicing discipleship principles that promote mental health and wellness.

Caring for Our Emotional Life

Emotions powerfully influence our thoughts, actions, and relationships. To live a spiritually fulfilling life, believers must surrender their emotions to God. By doing so, they can navigate life's inevitable ups and downs with faith and confidence in Christ. Martin Manser highlights the significance of emotions in believers' decisions and actions: "Scripture portrays both human beings and God as having emotions. Human emotions and sentiments are of importance to the life of faith. Human feelings can be positive or negative and are subject to change and misinterpretation."[293] Navigating one's emotions by submitting them to God brings positive results. Biblical emotions include love, compassion, joy, delight, anger, sorrow, pain, and fear. God created us to have emotional responses to situations, but mature believers also examine the appropriateness of their emotional responses. Having emotions is neither positive nor negative, but if we do not keep our reactions in check, we risk letting a response fester into sin.

Emotional health comes from submission to Christ and the Word of God. Ryan S. Peterson promotes a holistic walk with God that balances conflicting emotions: "The ideal state is one in which a person's reason, emotions, and desires submit to God and act in harmony with one another. … When we find ourselves experiencing repeated patterns of anxiety, lack of gratitude, and conflict, we are called back to God."[294] The spiritual discipline of aligning one's emotions with God's character and Word requires turning back to Him. By relying on the foundation of God's Word, one can quickly restore peace amidst turmoil.

Developing emotional intelligence is an important aspect of spiritual maturity. David Brown insightfully discusses how Jesus set the standard of emotional intelligence and "real humanity" when He, too, was deeply moved and wept at the news from Mary and Martha that their brother Lazarus had died (John 11:17-38).[295] In response to their anguish and His own, He raises Lazarus from the dead, increasing the faith of all who witnessed the event (vv. 38-44). It remains critical to align emotions with God's character and Word. Healthy emotions reflect God's image, elevating a positive influence in the world and strengthening the body of Christ.

Managing emotions is vital for healthy living. As Charlie Self states, emotions can be managed through strategies after analyzing, discerning their origins, and understanding how they affect behavior. Self gives various reasons for negative emotions, including "feelings of guilt for some sin, a sense of abandonment, anticipation of danger or death, a fear of the future, and many more reasons. It is not possible to avoid negative emotions. Disciples do not ignore or deny that they experience negative emotions. Disciples learn to manage negative emotions."[296] Turning toward our emotions allows us to invite the Holy Spirit to begin the healing process. Cultivating healthy emotions involves understanding and managing the underlying causes of emotions. When we experience emotions such as sorrow, grief, or depression, we need to explore and evaluate these feelings.

We may benefit from counseling with a trusted relationship to cultivate healthy emotions. Research reveals that ongoing and regular communication can bring emotional health and well-being to individuals in recovery. Mentor/mentee interactions are critical to successful recovery programs, and effective communication is an absolute must for achieving the desired outcomes. These interactions help to establish healthy communication patterns, promote accountability, and foster trust. Having a sponsor or mentor, according to research conducted by Angelo Messina, can help promote emotional health and reduce the likelihood of recidivism. Messina notes that people recovering from addiction benefited from mentors in two primary ways: "First, they experienced their mentor as someone with whom they could confide. Second, they experienced their mentor as someone who supported them. Support from mentors took different forms, from emotional support to meeting essential needs."[297] The emotional impact of trust and encouragement from sponsors or mentors can have long-lasting effects on the recovery community, significantly aiding the pursuit of a sober lifestyle.

Caring for the Body

Care for the body remains critical for holistic health. The concept of the body in Scripture can refer to one's physical being, or it can be used figuratively. As Jonathon Lookadoo notes, Scripture uses a variety of terms to refer to the "physical body, but they may also be used figuratively with moral or theological implications. The tongue can refer to speech (Ps 12:3; Jas 1:26); the heart can refer to the entirety of one's desires (Rom 1:24); the arm can represent power and authority (Isa 59:1)."[298] Christian Wolf adds that the Old Testament's view of the body (*basar*) is typically translated as "flesh" and is associated with being "mortal, with physical needs, weak and subject to temptation."[299] The body is a temporary dwelling needed for worshipping God, building the Kingdom, and sharing the love of Christ with others.

Walter A. Elwell and Phillip Comfort rightly call attention to the spiritual development of the body, which involves a life of sacrifice: "Paul told Christians to present their bodies as a living sacrifice (Rom 12:1). Each individual human life is to be a 'living sacrifice' to God."[300] Although the body can be used for sinful purposes, it was designed as an instrument of worship and a dwelling place for the Holy Spirit. Paul emphasized the importance of glorifying God with the body: "Your body is the temple of the Holy Spirit. … You were bought with a price. Therefore, glorify God in your body and in your spirit, which are God's" (1 Cor 6:19–20).

The proper care and management of the body have a significant impact on the church. First, as mentioned in 1 Corinthians 6, our bodies are considered sacred temples that contain the divine presence of God. Therefore, we must prioritize physical well-being because it plays a crucial role in fostering and maintaining a spiritual connection with God. As followers of Christ, who are called to reflect His character, many people aim to develop a godly image that encourages and motivates them. By caring for their bodies, individuals can improve their lives and serve as positive examples for others.

When I was younger, I used to smoke cigarettes. Then one day I had a vision of people smoking in the pews of my home church. I was angry at their lack of concern for the house of God. In the vision, I went through the church, grabbing cigarettes from everyone and snuffing them out. I stopped at the front and said, "What do you think you are doing? Don't you know this is the house of God?" Immediately, I heard the Lord say to me, "This is how I feel about you. Don't you know you are the temple of God? You were bought at a price. You are not your own." I don't tell this story to shame anyone who smokes. I only tell it because this was how God revealed to me that I could no longer smoke where He wanted to use me.

Our physical health influences how we can become part of the body of Christ, which is an essential step for the recovery community. The life of someone with an addiction is often marked by independence and reliance on survival skills. However, living in a community of Christ-like followers can offer a sense of shared purpose and common focus. Addiction can be a destructive force that not only impacts a person's health but also their social life. It can lead to feelings of loneliness and isolation, causing them to develop survival strategies. Being part of a community is vital for a person's growth as a member of the Body. The Apostle Paul emphasizes the importance of belonging to the Body and fulfilling one's role. According to Scripture, Christ is the head of the Body, the Church. This analogy is essential for understanding the relationship between Christians and their fellow believers. Moreover, our gifts can only serve God and the Church by serving each other with our bodies. Christians are accountable for the well-being of the community of believers, the body of Christ, by utilizing their gifts and serving each other with love.

Disciplines

Examen

Examen is a discipline that we must not overlook as we seek holistic health. Examination of oneself is essential for repentance and for acknowledging our need for the Savior. The spiritual discipline used by the ancient fathers is the Prayer of Examen. Richard Foster explains the basics of the Prayer of Examen, which has two parts, the examen of consciousness and the examen of conscience. The examen of consciousness is an outward focus on God's presence, in which we ask, "How was God with me today, and how did I respond to Him?" The examen of conscience, meanwhile, is inward focused on our sins, our distortions, and where we need healing. We examine ourselves and ask, "Where do I need cleansing, purifying, or transformation?"[301] Foster explains that both questions are part of the Prayer of Examen: "The examen of consciousness and the examen of conscience are a little like the waves of the ocean: distinct from one another and yet constantly on top of and never totally separate from each other."[302] Foster adds that we can pay attention to God and ourselves through various means such as journaling or documenting "how God speaks through the course of ordinary events."[303]

Cathie Macaulay emphasizes that the Examen is an exercise of discipleship, one in which we "share in the Passion and Resurrection of Christ and the spiritual movements and choices within each person's everyday lives."[304] A sample Daily Examen that we can practice morning and evening can be as simple as following these steps: "Become aware of God's presence. Review the day with gratitude. Pay attention to your emotions. Choose one feature of the day and pray from it. Look toward tomorrow."[305] Daily reflection helps us find God and consider how we may have missed Him throughout the day's interactions. Examen is a practice of self-correction, resolutions, and reflection. Examen is a tool to discover oneself and one's relationship to the Father. We must not overlook the value of spending daily time to meditate on the actions, thoughts, and attitudes of our day.

Solitude

Another important discipline for holistic health is solitude. Jesus regularly retreated to spend time with the Father. As Richard Foster notes, Jesus began His ministry in solitude (Matt 4:1-11) and retreated in solitude before selecting His disciples (Luke 6:12), after feeding the multitudes (Matt 14:23), after ministering to others (Mark 1:35; 6:31), and "as he prepared for his highest and most holy work ... (Matt 26:36–46)," among multiple other times.[306] Foster also notes that solitude is a matter of listening and careful attentiveness to the Father:

> We can cultivate an inner solitude and silence that sets us free from loneliness and fear. Loneliness is inner emptiness. Solitude is inner fulfillment. Solitude is more a state of mind and heart than it is a place. There is a solitude of the

heart that can be maintained at all times. Crowds, or the lack of them, have little to do with this inward attentiveness. It is quite possible to be a desert hermit and never experience solitude. But if we possess inward solitude we do not fear being alone, for we know that we are not alone. Neither do we fear being with others, for they do not control us. In the midst of noise and confusion we are settled into a deep inner silence. Whether alone or among people, we always carry with us a portable sanctuary of the heart.[307]

Though Jesus practiced solitude, He did not always retreat alone. He told His disciples after a particularly busy day of ministry to "come with me by yourselves to a quiet place and get some rest" (Mark 6:31–32).

Alicia Britt Chole writes poetically about retreating as a regular practice for health and wholeness: "Jesus's example grants us permission (and perhaps even a directive) to retreat to a solitary place for extended prayer. Think of prayer retreating as a scheduled rain for your reservoir. Living water from heaven refills us as we enjoy Jesus's company on long walks or delight in Jesus's artistry in the canvas of the sky."[308] Would you consider with me that retreating is a valid form of spiritual formation and one that is often overlooked in our busy lives? If we started our relationship with Jesus in a beautiful, intimate moment, how much more do we want to return to that when we are tired and worn from busyness and distractions? We must intentionally turn aside towards solitary moments with Christ.

Creative Encounter

What does the best version of you look like? Filled, skilled, and serving? Using an abandoned hymnal or Bible, construct a paragraph using phrases to describe your whole, healed life. Glue the  words into a journal to remind you of God's desires for a whole and reconciled life.

An additional creative activity is called Words of My Mouth. We used to do something like this in grade school when we would cut a silhouette of ourselves from black construction paper. This encounter starts with sketching your profile silhouette on a canvas. You will need a buddy for the first part. Hold your canvas next to your shoulder where the shadow falls from your head onto the canvas.

Then ask a friend to use their phone light (or another light source) to cast a shadow of your head onto the canvas, and have your friend trace your profile onto the canvas. You can then paint the silhouette in different colors or collage images inside the profile to describe you. From there, adhere text from magazines, Bible verses, or songs emerging from the mouth of the silhouette. Use Mod podge and your foam sponge to attach the images and texts.

Your words have influence and meaning. What words are coming out of your mouth to build the likeness of Christ in you? Remember that our focus is simply to process our words and situations with the Spirit.

Application

Habit formation is essential for building discipline and achieving long-lasting change. Habit formation involves identifying our triggers that lead to unhealthy habits and replacing them with positive ones that align with our values and goals. You can make only so many decisions in a single day. Some people wear the same outfit every day just to avoid deciding. Wendy Wood writes brilliantly about habits, decisions, and how to make changes in one's life. She encourages us to make a plan and stick to it. Use your frontal lobe, the executive decision maker, to make the commitment and then do not re-negotiate it: "Skip the debate chamber and get to work. That's exactly what habits are for."[309] She adds, "You have to somehow become committed to the consistent procedures of doing things."[310]

By consistently practicing healthy habits, we can establish a solid foundation for personal growth and development. Habit formation is a long-lasting tool for healthy living. Chandler observes that, as biblical habits are put into practice, "our identity as sons and daughters of God is affirmed through spiritual practices that reinforce the grand narrative of our faith through godly virtues that exemplify kingdom ethics."[311] The power of the mind to shape an individual's physical and emotional states is undeniable.

Reframing our mindset can have a significant impact on our overall well-being. Paul uses physical training as an analogy to explain that, although he focuses on training his body, his main goal is spiritual growth (1 Cor 9:25-27). This involves following a routine of proper nutrition, mobility exercises, and mindful dietary intake. By keeping the physical body healthy, believers can better serve the Kingdom and steward their bodies well. Regular exercise and healthy eating habits in maintaining a healthy body and mind are essential for stewardship.

Body image can become corrupted based on the choices and the company we keep, which can have a negative impact on our overall physical health. To mitigate this, we can start by cultivating a positive self-image and adopting healthy habits through the power of the Holy Spirit. Ultimately, sustained success requires us to prioritize our physical health and cultivate life skills that promote overall well-being. The process of habit formation is instrumental in building godly character and supporting positive change and full potential. Small daily routines add up. Make your bed! Shine your sink!

Holistic spiritual formation is a comprehensive process that involves nurturing and strengthening every part of us, including the spirit, soul, mind, emotions, and body. Ignoring or neglecting any of these areas can lead to imbalance, both spiritually and physically. However, when every part of us is shaped and transformed through the teachings of the Word of God, the likeness of Christ becomes more visible in humanity. This deliberate approach to addressing each aspect of our being can bring spiritual freedom and help us live a God-centered life.

Conclusion

When I began searching for help, I was desperate for sobriety. The truth is that my husband told me that if I continued to choose drugs over him and the boys, I would need to find a new home, and my mother wouldn't let me stay at her house. I called the local Teen Challenge center. At that time in Arizona, Teen Challenge had only homes for girls under seventeen and a men's facility, but they didn't offer any programs for women or moms with kids. I had no place to go. Today, Adult and Teen Challenge have programs for both women and men, as well as teenagers. Even though I couldn't access Teen Challenge at the time of my need in the 1990s, addiction recovery programs, and Teen Challenge in particular, remain close to my heart.

Thankfully, I had people I could turn to. My husband and church community rallied around me with supportive love. They were my lifeline 24/7 for many years. I remain forever thankful for my 90s support gang: Shelly, Rhonda, Donna, Tiffany, Dawn, Terri, Naomi, Margaret, Greta, Peggy, Joy, Gwyneth, and Shirley. Together we learned what sobriety looks like as we navigated the road to healing through Bible studies, friendships, and our close-knit community. Love bonded my church to me as they refused to give up on me. Their constant affirmations of biblical truth in love exposed me to Jesus.

I'm sorry if you have been overlooked and underserved as a Christian addict. You may be a God-fearing believer struggling with addiction, life-controlling issues, and unresolved trauma. And you deserve proper ministry and quality resources. Jesus sees you.

I have a message for you—don't give up. Don't give up on your pastor, their spouse, the church community, or God. Maybe the history you bring with you is a brand-new concept for your church community. Maybe they don't quite know what to do with you! As you head toward freedom and recovery, bring the church with you. You may need to be extra vulnerable and invite them to your healing party. Teach the church how to love and support you. Be brave through taking initiative. Be a bridge for others to come after you. Now is the time to make a difference in your community.

Perhaps the pastor needs assistance launching a recovery support group. You could be the very person to spark this group into action. In Chapter 7, we discussed the image of a witness. Ask God to give you a platform to stand on so you can share your recovery testimony. Or simply pick an evening that works, make a pot of decaf coffee, and use this book as a twelve-session test pilot with a group of like-minded sobriety warriors.

The biblical figures we studied taught us lessons of spiritual growth through their journeys, challenges, and adventures. Chances are, one of the characters made a big impact on your thinking. I encourage you to remember the images, associated characters, and creative encounters so God can continue to shape and spiritually mature you. Make space for creativity with God.

In closing, I pray that the words of the Apostle Paul become our message and marching orders:

> Therefore, if anyone is in Christ, the new creation has come: The old has gone, the new is here! All this is from God, who reconciled us to himself through Christ and gave us the ministry of reconciliation: that God was reconciling the world to himself in Christ, not counting people's sins against them. And he has committed to us the message of reconciliation. We are therefore Christ's ambassadors, as though God were making his appeal through us. We implore you on Christ's behalf: Be reconciled to God.

God made him who had no sin to be sin for us, so that in him we might become the righteousness of God (2 Cor 5:16).

You are a creative, adventurous minister of reconciliation! Let's do this!

ACKNOWLEDGEMENTS

Heavenly Father, I know and love you more than ever. I love that You created me spunky, artistic, and adventurous. You have called me out of darkness for my good and Your glory. I'm so happy to have been on this learning journey with You. You invited me to swim in deeper water, although I wanted to stay on the seashore collecting shells. You told me I would see greater things if I would launch into the deep, where I would be doing things I could never imagine. Boy, that was an understatement! I'm so thankful I chose to follow You. Your faithful provision of daily manna will never be forgotten. After a resting season, let's do another grand adventure!

To my godly husband who is my best friend, your love for God allowed me to fulfill this assignment. Your constant blessings and anointing kept me encouraged. Thank you for keeping the supplements and coffee coming. I am a better version of myself because of you. I acknowledge the sacrifices and unintended consequences of this season. We heard from God, said "Yes," and have been carried all the way.

My loving children, I want to especially acknowledge you. Thank you for giving me breadth and space to lean into this season of academia. My seven sweet grandcuties, MiMi is done! Now we can have adventures again.

My dear friends who prayed and interceded for me as I worked on papers, thank you for serenading me with cheers. Your words were sweet breaths of refreshment.

My church family, Oracle Assembly, I am honored to have you all in my life. Thank you for stepping up and taking on some of the work for the house of God, giving me the opportunity and time to read and write.

The kingdom of God is advancing and exploding because of the professors and leaders involved in my DMin. educational journey. This includes John Battaglia, Robert Eby, Brenda Reed, Vince Medina, Charlie Self, Cory Shipley, Carolyn Tennant, and Allen Tennison. Thank you for your intentionality and investments in me.

Erica Huinda, you are a beautiful gift to me. Thank you for lending your wonderful skills and for your availability. Thank you for swimming with me and keeping me from drowning.

ENDNOTES

1. "Jonesing" is slang for a craving or an "avid desire or appetite for something." *Merrian Webster Dictionary*, s.v. "jonesing," https://www.merriam-webster.com/dictionary/jones. Accessed Nov. 11, 2025.

2. Dallas Willard et al., *The Kingdom Life: A Practical Theology of Discipleship and Spiritual Formation,* ed. Alan Andrews (Nav Press., 2016), 48.

3. A. W. Tozer, *The Knowledge of the Holy* (Fig, 2017), 4.

4. Gordon J. Wenham et al., eds. "Genesis," in *New Bible Commentary*, 21st Century ed., 4th ed. (InterVarsity Press, 1994), 55.

5. Sandra L. Richter, *The Epic of Eden: A Christian Entry into the Old Testament* (IVP Academic 2008), 115, Kinde.

6. *Oxford English Dictionary*, s.v. "relationship," https://www.oed.com/search/dictionary/?scope=Entries&q=relationship.

7. John Skinner, *A Critical and Exegetical Commentary on Genesis* (Scribner, 1910), The Creation of Animals, Logos.

8. Skinner, *A Critical and Exegetical Commentary on Genesis*, 31.

9. Brannon Ellis et al., s.v. "angels," *Lexham Survey of Theology* (Faithlife Corporation, 2018), Logos Bible Software.

10. Mark E. Biddle et al., s.v. *"selem," Theological Lexicon of the Old Testament* (Hendrickson Publisher, 1997), Logos.

11. Richter, *The Epic of Eden*, 107.

12. Allen C. Myers, "Image of God," in *The Eerdmans Bible Dictionary* (Eerdmans, 1987), 516, Logos.

13. Laird Harris et al., eds., s.v. "(צֶלֶם *selem*)," *Theological Wordbook of the Old Testament,* electronic ed. (Moody Press, 1999), 768, Logos.

14. Bria Burns, "Humanity's Original Integrity," in *Lexham Survey of Theology*, eds. Mark Ward, et al. (Lexham Press, 2018), The Doctrine of Humanity, Logos.

15. Zachary Lycans, "Sin and Death," in *Lexham Survey of Theology*, eds. Mark Ward et al. (Lexham Press, 2018), section 4, Logos.

16. Jerry A. Johnson, "Image of God," in *Holman Illustrated Bible Dictionary*, eds. Chad Brand, et al. (Holman Bible Publishers, 2003), 807, Logos.

17. Matthew Philipp Whelan, "Until Dignity Becomes Ordinary: The Grammar of Dignity in Catholic Social Teaching," *Religions* 14, no. 6 (2023):716, https://www.mdpi.com/2077-1444/14/6/716#B20-religions-14-00716.

18. Walter A. Elwell and Philip Wesley Comfort, s.v. "image of God," *Tyndale Bible Dictionary*, Tyndale Reference Library (Tyndale House Publishers, 2001), 627, Logos.

19. "Enuma Elish: The Epic of Creation," trans. Leonard W. King, in *The Seven Tablets of Creation*. 1902, https://sacred-texts.com/ane/enuma.htm

20. Michael S. Heiser, "Mesopotamian Creation Myths," in *The Lexham Bible Dictionary*, eds. John D. Barry, et al. (Lexham Press, 2016), Logos.

21. "Enuma Elish: The Epic of Creation."

22. Michael S. Heiser, "Image of God," in *The Lexham Bible Dictionary*, eds., John D. Barry et al. (Lexham Press, 2016), Logos.

23. Heiser, "Image of God."

24. Christopher J. H. Wright, *The Mission of God: Unlocking the Bible's Grand Narrative* (IVP Academic, 2006), 164.

25. Kevin R. Hoffman, "Developing a Faith-based Early Intervention Program for Adults with Alcohol and Drug Issues" (DMin project, Assemblies of God Theological Seminary, Springfield, MO, 2016), 42, ProQuest.

26. Larry L. Walker and Elmer A. Martens, *Isaiah, Jeremiah, & Lamentations*, vol. 8 of *Cornerstone Biblical Commentary* (Tyndale House Publishers, 2005), 12, Logos.

27. Brian S. Rosner, "The Concept of Idolatry," *Themelios* 24, no. 3 (May 1999): 21, https://www.thegospelcoalition.org/themelios/article/the-concept-of-idolatry.

28. Michael J. Ovey, "The Echo Chamber of Idolatry," *Themelios* 41, no. 2 (August 1, 2016): 214–16.

29. Allen P. Ross, "Genesis," in *The Bible Knowledge Commentary: An Exposition of the Scriptures*, eds. J. F. Walvoord and R. B. Zuck (Victor Books, 1985), 1:32, Logos.

30. Tremper Longman III and Peter Enns, *Dictionary of the Old Testament: Wisdom, Poetry, and Writings* (InterVarsity Press, 2008), 194.

31. Stanley E. Porter, s.v. "παρὰ," *Idioms of the Greek New Testament* (JSOT Press, 1999), Logos Bible Software.

32. Ernst Harald Riesenfeld, s.v. "παρὰ," *Theological Dictionary of the New Testament*, eds. Gerhard Kittel et al., electronic ed. (Eerdmans, 1964), 5:735, Logos.

33. Johannes P. Louw and Eugene Albert Nida, s.v. "σεβάζομαι," *Greek-English Lexicon of the New Testament: Based on Semantic Domains*, 2nd ed. (United Bible Societies, 1996), 1:539, Logos.

34. Joseph Henry Thayer, s.v. "παρὰ," *A Greek-English Lexicon of the New Testament: Being Grimm's Wilke's Clavis Novi Testamenti* (Harper & Brothers,1889), 478.

35. William Sanday and Arthur C. Headlam, *A Critical and Exegetical Commentary on the Epistle of the Romans*, 3rd ed. International Critical Commentary (C. Scribner's Sons, 1897), 44, Logos.

36. Deborah Sokolove, "The Work of Visual Art in Liturgy," *Studia Liturgica* (2022), https://doi.org/10.1177/00393207221075753.

37. Gary Thomas, *Sacred Pathways: Nine Ways to Connect with God* (Zondervan, 2020), 178-179.

38. BBC Radio, "Turning to Art," *Four Thought*, February 1, 2023, https://www.bbc.com/audio/play/m001hpbb. See also Ted Harrison, "Religion and Art." *Theology*, (2023). Accessed January 7, 2026. https://doi.org/10.1177/0040571X231161733.

39. Beat Rink, "Art from a Christian Point of View," *ArtWay* (October 2010), https://www.artway.eu/posts/art-from-a-christian-point-of-view.

40. Rink, "Art from a Christian Point of View."

41. Jessa E. Hernandez et al., "Learning Styles/Preferences among Medical Students: Kinesthetic Learner's Multimodal Approach to Learning Anatomy," *Medical Science Educator* 30, no. 4 (Aug 2020): 1633-1634, https://pubmed.ncbi.nlm.nih.gov/34457831/.

42. "Kinesthetic Strategies," VARK Learn Ltd., accessed October 3, 2025, https://vark-learn.com/strategies/kinesthetic-strategies/.

43. Giffin Gooch, "Building a Universalized Theory for Spiritual Disciplines: Beyond Denomination, Personality, and Socio-Historical Experience," *Journal of Spiritual Formation and Soul Care* 17, no. 2 (2024): 411, https://doi.org/10.1177/19397909241256904.

44. Michael L. Humphries, "Imagery," in *Eerdmans Dictionary of the Bible*, eds. David Noel Freedman, et al. (W. B. Eerdmans, 2000), 633, Logos Bible Software.

45. David Seal, "Parable," in *The Lexham Bible Dictionary*, eds. John D. Barry, et al. (Lexham Press, 2016), Logos Bible Software.

46. All Scripture quotations, unless otherwise noted, are from the NIV.

47. Allen C. Myers, s.v. "halakhah," in *The Eerdmans Bible Dictionary*, (Eerdmans, 1987), 455, Logos.

48. David M. Rosenberg, "Glossary of Certain Terms Relevant to Orthodox Life," JCFS Chicago, (2022) 2, https://www.jcfs.org/sites/default/files/inline-files/Glossary%20of%20certain%20terms%20relevant%20to%20Orthodox%20Life%202022.pdf

49. Rabbi Meir, "Teaching Torah through Meshalim Halachah and Aggadah," https://rmbhcharities.com/rabbi-meir-resources/torah-teachings/three-parts.

50. Mike Dowgiewicz and Sue Dowgiewicz, "Prodigal Church: My Will, My Way, My Glory," (Restoration Ministries, 2022), 22.

51. Christopher J. H. Wright, *The Mission of God: Unlocking the Bible's Grand Narrative* (InterVarsity Press, 2013), 1055, Kindle Edition.

52. Ronald E. Clements, " ".אַבְרָהָם In *Theological Dictionary of the Old Testament*, edited by G. Johannes Botterweck and Helmer Ringgren, translated by John T. Willis, Revised Edition, (Eerdmans Publishing Company, 1977), 1:55, Logos Bible Software.

53. John H. Walton et al., *The IVP Bible Background Commentary: Old Testament* (InterVarsity Press, 2012), 46, Kindle.

54. F. B. Huey, "Patriarchs," in *Holman Concise Bible Commentary*, ed. David S. Dockery (Broadman & Holman Publishers, 1998), 18, Logos Bible Software.

55. John A. Beck, "Altars, Tombs, Pillars, and Wells in Genesis: Their Socio-Spatial and Theological Roles" in *Lexham Geographic Commentary on the Pentateuch*, ed. Barry J. Beitzel (Lexham Press, 2022), Logos Bible Software.

56. Walton et al., *The IVP Bible Background Commentary: Old Testament*, 66.

57. James Hastings et al., "Machpelah," in *Dictionary of the Bible* (Charles Scribner's Sons, 1909), 564, Logos Bible Software.

58. Walton et al., *The IVP Bible Background Commentary: Old Testament*, 43.

59. Ronald E. Clements, " ",אַבְרָהָם in *Theological Dictionary of the Old Testament*, vol. 1, ed. G. Johannes Botterweck and Helmer Ringgren (Eerdmans, 1974).

60. Wright, *The Mission of God*, 742.

61. Evan B. Howard, *A Guide to Christian Spiritual Formation: How Scripture, Spirit, Community, and Mission Shape Our Souls* (Baker Publishing Group, 2018), 85, Kindle.

62. Gary Hardin, "Obedience," in *Holman Illustrated Bible Dictionary*, eds. Chad Brand et al. (Holman Bible Publishers, 2003), 1206, Logos.

63. Wendy Buttacy, *Breaking Free*, Personal Studies for New Life in Christ (Adult & Teen Challenge U.S.A., 2019), 14.

64. Wright, *Mission*, 163.

65. Kyle Idleman, *Gods at War: Defeating the Idols that Battle for Your Heart* (Zondervan, 2013), 381–427, Kindle Edition.

66. Adult and Teen Challenge, PSNL Personal Self-Evaluation Worksheet, https://store.teenchallengeusa.org/psnl-personal-self-evaluation-worksheet-50-pk/.

67. Gregory K. Beale, *We Become What We Worship: A Biblical Theology of Idolatry* (IVP, 2009), 16, Kindle.

68. Don Allen Tennison, "Foundations of Spiritual Theology and Formation" (class notes from Core 4 class at Assemblies of God Theological Seminary, Springfield, MO, February 2024).

69. Tennison, "Foundations of Spiritual Theology and Formation."

70. Gary D. Baldwin, "Jacob," in *Holman Illustrated Bible Dictionary*, eds. Chad Brand et al. (Holman Bible Publishers, 2003), 864, Logos.

71. Baldwin, "Jacob," 864.

72. *Merriam-Webster Dictionary*, s.v. "struggle," https://www.merriam-webster.com/dictionary/struggle.

73. John Skinner, "Jacob's Flight from Laban: Their Friendly Parting," in *A Critical and Exegetical Commentary on Genesis*, International Critical Commentary (Scribner, 1910), 1851-1925.

74. John H. Walton et al., *The IVP Bible Background Commentary: Old Testament* (InterVarsity Press, 2014), 65, Kindle Edition.

75. Watchman Nee, *Changed into His Likeness* (CLC Publications, 2012), 1355, Kindle Edition.

76. Nee, *Changed into His Likeness*, 1553.

77. U.S. Centers for Disease Control and Prevention, "Epigenetics, Health, and Disease," https://www.cdc.gov/genomics-and-health/epigenetics/index.ht ml

78. Caroline Leaf, *Think, Learn, Succeed: Understanding and Using Your Mind to Thrive at School, the Workplace, and Life* (Baker Books, 2018), 37, Kindle Edition.

79. Daniel Amen, *Your Brain Is Always Listening: Tame the Hidden Dragons That Control Your Happiness, Habits, and Hang-Ups* (Tyndale, 2021), 98, Kindle.

80. Charlie Self et al., *Life in 5D: A New Vision of Discipleship* (5D Press, 2022), 82.

81. Amen, *Your Brain Is Always Listening*, 99.

82. Gary Thomas, *Sacred Pathways: Nine Ways to Connect with God* (Zondervan, 2020), 34.

83. Thomas, *Sacred Pathways*, 63.

84. Caroline Leaf, *Think, Learn, Succeed*, 59, Kindle Edition.

85. Shelly J. Hogan, "The Supernatural Work of Forgiveness, Repentance, and Reconciliation: A Ministry Strategy for the Body of Christ to Facilitate Inner Healing and Freedom from Strongholds" (DMin project, AGTS, Springfield, MO, 2017), 61, ProQuest.

86. *World Book Encyclopedia*, s.v. "Butterfly," vol. 2 (World Book, Inc, 2022), 741.

87. National Geographic, "Salmon," https://www.nationalgeographic.com/animals/fish/facts/salmon.

88. Isaiah Hoogendyk, ed., s.v. "ascent," *The Lexham Analytical Lexicon of the Hebrew Bible* (Lexham Press, 2017), Kindle.

89. Don Allen Tennison, "Foundations of Spiritual Theology and Formation" (class notes from Core 4 class at Assemblies of God Theological Seminary, Springfield, MO, February 2024).

90. Eugene Carpenter, *Exodus*, vol. 1 of *Evangelical Exegetical Commentary* (Lexham Press, 2016), Ex 2:10, Logos.

91. Allen C. Myers, "Moses," in *The Eerdmans Bible Dictionary* (Eerdmans, 1987), 731, Logos.

92. Dewayne Bryant, "Egypt, Religion of," in *The Lexham Bible Dictionary*, eds. John D. Barry et al. (Lexham Press, 2016), Logos.

93. Cecil P. Staton, Jr. "Theophany," in *Eerdmans Dictionary of the Bible*, ed. David Noel Freedman, et al. (W. B. Eerdmans, 2000), 1298, Logos.

94. See Exod 13:21–22; Gen 16:7–13; 18; 1 Kgs 19.

95. Theodore Hiebert, "Theophany in the OT," in *The Anchor Yale Bible Dictionary*, ed. David Noel Freedman (Doubleday, 1992) 6:505, Logos.

96. John H. Walton et al., *The IVP Bible Background Commentary: Old Testament* (IVP Academic, 2012), 171, Kindle Edition.

97. Warren W. Wiersbe, s.v. "Exodus 32:7–14," *Wiersbe's Expository Outlines on the Old Testament* (Victor Books, 1993), Logos.

98. Eugene H. Merrill, "Numbers," in *The Bible Knowledge Commentary: An Exposition of the Scriptures*, eds. J. F. Walvoord and R. B. Zuck (Victor Books, 1985) 1:231, Logos.

99. Diane Swanson, *Forgiveness: A Workbook on Why and How to Forgive* (CreateSpace, 2015), 29.

100. Shelly Hogan, seminar notes, E5 Conference, November 6, 2026, Dubois, PA.

101. Malcolm Brubaker, "Corrie ten Boom: Habakkuk's Companion in Doubt," in *They Spoke from God: A Survey of the Old Testament*, eds. William C. Williams and Stanley M. Horton (Gospel Publishing House, 2003), 780, Logos.

102. United States Holocaust Memorial Museum, "Introduction to the Holocaust," *Holocaust Encyclopedia*, https://encyclopedia.ushmm.org/content/en/article/introduction -to-the-holocaust, accessed November 18, 2025.

103. Corrie ten Boom, "Corrie ten Boom on Forgiveness," Guideposts Classics, https://guideposts.org/positive-living/guideposts-classics-corrie-ten-boom-forgiveness/

104. ten Boom, "Corrie ten Boom on Forgiveness."

105. William Arndt et al., s.v. "forgiving," *A Greek-English Lexicon of the New Testament and Other Early Christian Literature*, 3rd ed. (University of Chicago Press, 2000), 1078, Logos.

106. Caroline Leaf, *Think, Learn, Succeed: Understanding and Using Your Mind to Thrive at School, the Workplace, and Life* (Baker Books, 2018), 70, Kindle Edition.

107. Neil T. Anderson, *Winning Spiritual Warfare* (Harvest Pocket Books, 1990), 282, Kindle.

108. Anderson, *Winning Spiritual Warfare*, 282.

109. Evan Howard, *A Guide to Christian Spiritual Formation* (Baker, 2018), 34.

110. Craig S. Keener, *The IVP Bible Background Commentary: New Testament* (InterVarsity Press, 2014), 187, Kindle.

111. Keener, *The IVP Bible Background Commentary: New Testament*, 187.

112. Risto Uro, *Ritual and Christian Beginning* (Oxford University Press, 2018), 85.

113. Benjamin J. Snyder, s.v. "mikvah," *The Lexham Bible Dictionary*, eds. John D. Barry et al. (Lexham Press, 2016), Logos.

114. Snyder, s.v. "mikvah."

115. Snyder, s.v. "mikvah."

116. Don Allen Tennison, "Foundations of Spiritual Theology and Formation" (class notes from Core 4 class at Assemblies of God Theological Seminary, Springfield, MO, February 2024).

117. Ithamar Gruenwald, "The Baptism of Jesus in Light of Jewish Ritual Practice," in *Neotestametica* 50, no. 2 (New Testament Society of Southern Africa, 2016), 311, https://www.academia.edu/42943720/Ithamar_Gruenwald_The_Baptism_of_Jesus_in_Light_of_Jewish_Ritual_Practice_Neotestamentica_vol_50_no_2_2016_301_325.

118. Snyder, s.v. "mikvah."

119. Peter Kirby, "Historical Jesus Theories," Early Christian Writings, 2026, accessed January 15, 2026, http://www.earlychristianwritings.com/text/1clement-hoole.html.

120. Keener, *The IVP Bible Background Commentary: New Testament*, 52.

121. Lesley DiFransico, "Repentance," in *Lexham Theological Wordbook*, eds. Douglas Mangum et al., Lexham Bible Reference Series (Lexham Press, 2014), Theological Overview, Logos.

122. David J. A. Clines, ed., " ",שׁוּב in *The Dictionary of Classical Hebrew* (Sheffield Phoenix Press, 1993–2011), 8:273, Logos.

123. Wayne Dehoney, "Acts," in *The Teacher's Bible Commentary*, eds. H. Franklin Paschall and Herschel H. Hobbs (Broadman and Holman Publishers, 1972), 694, Logos.

124. Dehoney, "Acts," 292.

125. James Hastings et al., s.v. "Uncleanliness in the Old Testament," in *Dictionary of the Bible* (Charles Scribner's Sons, 1909), 144, Logos.

126. Wendy Buttacy, *Breaking Free: Confronting Toxic Denial*, Personal Studies for New Life in Christ Series (Adult & Teen Challenge, 2019), 4.

127. William Rinn et al., "Addiction Denial and Cognitive Dysfunction: A Preliminary Investigation," *The Journal of Neuropsychiatry and Clinical Neurosciences* 14, no. 1 (February 2002): 52, https://psychiatryonline.org/doi/full/10.1176/jnp.14.1.52.

128. Rinn et al., "Addiction Denial and Cognitive Dysfunction," 52.

129. Rinn et al., "Addiction Denial and Cognitive Dysfunction," 52-53.

130. Rinn et al., "Addiction Denial and Cognitive Dysfunction," 56.

131. Charity Anderson, "Addiction Denial: Symptoms, Behaviors and How to Help," American Addiction Centers, April 1, 2025, https://americanaddictioncenters.org/rehab-guide/addiction-denial.

132. Anderson, "Addiction Denial."

133. Towns, *Fasting for Spiritual Breakthrough*, Step 7.

134. Towns, *Fasting for Spiritual Breakthrough*, Step 7.

135. Towns, *Fasting for Spiritual Breakthrough*, Step 7.

136. General Council of the Assemblies of God, "06. The Ordinances of the Church," Assemblies of God Statement of Fundamental Truths, https://ag.org/beliefs/statement-of-fundamental-truths.

137. Martin H. Manser, s.v. "servanthood," *Dictionary of Bible Themes: The Accessible and Comprehensive Tool for Topical Studies* (Martin Manser, 2009), Logos.

138. Johannes P. Louw and Eugene Albert Nida, s.v. "helper," *Greek-English Lexicon of the New Testament: Based on Semantic Domains*, electronic ed. of the 2nd ed. (United Bible Societies, 1996), 1:459, Logos.

139. Nijay K. Gupta, "Christology," in *The Lexham Bible Dictionary* (Lexham Press, 2016), Logos.

140. Warren W. Wiersbe, *The Bible Exposition Commentary*, vol. 2 (Victor Books, 1996), Phil. 2, Logos.

141. Robert P. Lightner, "Philippians," in *The Bible Knowledge Commentary: An Exposition of the Scriptures*, eds. J. F. Walvoord and R. B. Zuck (Victor Books, 1985), 2:654, Logos.

142. Lightner, "Philippians," 2:653.

143. James Swanson and Orville Nave, s.v. "servanthood," *New Nave's Topical Bible* (Logos Research Systems, 1994), Logos.

144. Craig S. Keener, *The IVP Bible Background Commentary: New Testament* (IVP, 2014), 96, Kindle.

145. D. R. Wood et al., s.v. "foot," *The New Bible Dictionary*, 3rd ed. (Universities and Colleges Christian Fellowship, 1996), Logos.

146. Eugene E. Carpenter and Philip W. Comfort, s.v. "wash," *Holman Treasury of Key Bible Words: 200 Greek and 200 Hebrew Words Defined and Explained* (Broadman & Holman Publishers, 2000), 415, Logos.

147. Carpenter and Comfort, s.v. "servant," *Holman Treasury of Key Bible Words*, 167.

148. Martin H. Manser, s.v. "servant," *Dictionary of Bible Themes: The Accessible and Comprehensive Tool for Topical Studies* (Martin Manser, 2009), Logos.

149. David A. Fryburg, "Kindness as a Stress Reduction-Health Promotion Intervention: A Review of the Psychobiology of Caring," *Am J Lifestyle Med* 16, no. 1 (January 2021): 89, https://pmc.ncbi.nlm.nih.gov/articles/PMC8848115/.

150. David R. Cregg and Jennifer S. Cheavens, "Healing through Helping: An Experimental Investigation of Kindness, Social Activities, and Reappraisal as Well-Being Interventions," *The Journal of Positive Psychology* 18, no. 6 (February 2022), https://doi.org/10.1080/17439760.2022.2154695.

151. Cregg and Cheavens, "Healing through Helping."

152. Cregg and Cheavens, "Healing through Helping."

153. Michael J. Poulin et al., "Giving to Others and the Association Between Stress and Mortality," *American Journal of Public Health* 103, no. 9 (September 2013), 1653.

154. Poulin et al., "Giving to Others," 1654.

155. Convoy of Hope, "About," https://convoyofhope.org/about/.

156. "Convoy of Hope Again Named to Forbes' 2025 List of America's Top Charities," PR Newswire, December. 12, 2025, https://www.prnewswire.com/news-releases/convoy-of-hope-again-named-to-forbes-2025-list-of-americas-top-charities-302640476.html.

157. Convoy of Hope, "Children's Feeding," https://convoyofhope.org/initiatives/childrens-feeding/.

158. Project Rescue, https://www.projectrescue.com.

159. Rebecca Shults, *The Healing Arts Workbook: Creative Interventions with at-Risk Populations* (Shults, 2023), 5, Kindle Edition.

160. Robert L. Woodson, *Lessons from the Least of These: The Woodson Principles* (Bombardier Books, 2020), 17, Kindle.

161. Kyle Idleman, *Gods at War: Defeating the Idols that Battle for Your Heart* (Zondervan, 2018), 1838, Kindle Edition.

162. Johannes P. Louw and Eugene Albert Nida, s.v. "witness," *Greek-English Lexicon of the New Testament: Based on Semantic Domains*, electronic ed. of the 2nd ed. (United Bible Societies, 1996), 1:417, Logos.

163. Stanley Horton, *Acts* (Gospel Publishing House, 1981), 140.

164. Horton, *Acts*, 41.

165. Wave Nunnally, *A Commentary on the Book of Acts* (n.p., 2007), 180.

166. Horton, *Acts*, 139.

167. Johannes P. Louw and Eugene Albert Nida, s.v. "wisdom," *Greek-English Lexicon of the New Testament: Based on Semantic Domains*, electronic ed. of the 2nd ed. (United Bible Societies, 1996), 1:383.

168. Nunally, *A Commentary on the Book of Acts*, 186.

169. John B. Polhill, "Acts," in *Holman Concise Bible Commentary*, ed. David S. Dockery (Broadman & Holman Publishers, 1998), 508-9, Logos.

170. Nunnally, *A Commentary on the Book of Acts*, 204.

171. Stefana Dan Laing, "Martyr," in *Holman Illustrated Bible Dictionary*, ed. Chad Brand, et al. (Holman Bible Publishers, 2003), 1085, Logos.

172. D. A. Carson, *Exegetical Fallacies* (Baker Academic, 1996), 36.

173. Paul A. Hartog, s.v. "martyr," *The Lexham Bible Dictionary*, eds. John D. Barry et al. (Lexham Press, 2016), Logos.

174. Hartog, s.v. "martyr."

175. Eugene Carpenter and Philip Comfort, s.v. "martyr," *Holman Treasury of Key Bible Words* (Holman Reference, 2000), 420.

176. Wayne Dehoney, "Acts," in *The Teacher's Bible Commentary*, ed. H. Franklin Paschall and Herschel H. Hobbs (Broadman and Holman Publishers, 1972), 693, Logos.

177. Nunnally, *A Commentary on the Book of Acts*, 185.

178. Horton, *Acts*, 42.

179. Horton, *Acts*, 41.

180. Robert L. Brandt and Zenas J. Bicket, *The Spirit Helps Us Pray: A Biblical Theology of Prayer* (Gospel Publishing House, 1993), 245.

181. Brandt and Bicket, *The Spirit Helps Us Pray*, 245.

182. David Neyland Sumarauw et al., "A Theological Review of Evangelism and Its Influence on Church Growth," *Journal of Indonesian Impressions* 4, no. 1 (January 2025): 1004.

183. Johannes Reimer, "Frangelism: Evangelizing by Storytelling," *Evangelical Review of Theology* 43, no. 3 (2019): 266, https://www.biblicalstudies.org.uk/pdf/evangelical-review-of-th eology/ert_43-3_263.pdf

184. Allen C. Myers, "Household," *The Eerdmans Bible Dictionary* (Eerdmans, 1987), 506, Logos.

185. Reimer, "Frangelism," 266.

186. Richard D. Oliver, *A Covocational Attitude: Sharing the Motivational Convictions of Paul* (pub. by author, 2025), 13, Kindle Edition.

187. Oliver, *Covocational*, 83.

188. Victor Ogunsola, "Digital Discipleship: Navigating the Opportunities and Challenges," Christian Missionary Foundation, April 29, 2025, https://cmfmission.org/digital-discipleship-navigating-the-oppo rtunities-and-challenges/.

189. Yakubu Jakada, "Gerontic Evangelism," *Great Commission Research Journal*, 14, no. 2 (2022): 111, https://place.asburyseminary.edu/gcrj/vol14/iss2/7/.

190. Sumarauw et al., "A Theological Review of Evangelism."

191. Wave Nunnally, *A Commentary on the Book of Acts* (Nunnally, 2007), 240.

192. Craig S. Keener, *Acts*, New Cambridge Bible Commentary, ed. Ben Witherington (Cambridge University, 2020), 277.

193. Craig S. Keener, *The IVP Bible Background Commentary: New Testament* (IVP Academic, 1993), 346, Kindle Edition.

194. F. F. Bruce, *Commentary on the Book of the Acts* (Marshall, Morgan and Scott, 1962), 201.

195. Bruce, *Commentary on the Book of the Acts*, 201.

196. Nunnally, *A Commentary on the Book of Acts*, 239.

197. William Arndt et al., s.v. "ἐκστάσει," *A Greek-English Lexicon of the New Testament and Other Early Christian Literature*, 3rd ed. (University of Chicago Press, 2000), 309, Logos.

198. Colin Kruse, *John*, vol. 4 of *Tyndale New Testament Commentaries* (Intervarsity Press, 2003), 129.

199. Kruse, *John*, 134.

200. David Brown et al., *Matthew-John*, vol. 5 of *A Commentary, Critical, Experimental, and Practical, on the Old and New Testaments* (William Collins, Sons, & Company, 1868), 22.

201. Tom Doyle, "I Found the Truth," April 23, 2020, https://unchartedministries.com/2020/04/23/i-found-the-truth/.

202. Doyle, "I Found the Truth."

203. Tom Doyle, *Dreams and Visions: Is Jesus Awakening the Muslim World?* (Tomas Nelson, 2012), 7, Kindle.

204. Doyle, *Dreams and Visions*, 15.

205. Gary Thomas, *Sacred Pathways: Nine Ways to Connect with God* (Zondervan, 2020), 34, Kindle Edition.

206. Sara Valentina Schieppati et al., "Religious and Sacred Art: Recent Psychological Perspectives," *Ricerche di Psicologia* 45, no. 1 (2022): 6.

207. Thomas, *Sacred Pathways*, 95.

208. Joanna Burley, "Amma Theodora Revisited: Wisdom for the Twenty-first Century," *American Benedictine Review* (December 2024): 429.

209. Thomas, *Sacred Pathways*, 114.

210. Thomas, *Sacred Pathways*, 115.

211. Thomas, *Sacred Pathways*, 133.

212. Thomas, *Sacred Pathways*, 146.

213. Jacqueline Grey, "Worship: A Pentecostal Perspective," *Australasian Pentecostal Studies* 24, no. 1 (2023): 54.

214. Thomas, *Sacred Pathways*, 190–191.

215. John Coe, "The Controversy over Contemplation and Contemplative Prayer: A Historical, Theological, and Biblical Resolution," *Journal of Spiritual Formation & Soul Care* (Spring 2014): 150, 151.

216. Thomas, *Sacred Pathways*, 209.

217. Thomas, *Sacred Pathways*, 210.

218. Gary Tyra, *Introduction to Spirituality* (Baker Academic, 2023), 5.

219. Tyra, *Introduction to Spirituality*, 5.

220. Richard J. Foster, *Celebration of Discipline: The Path to Spiritual Growth* (Harper & Row Publishers, 1978), 96.

221. David Setran, *Spiritual Formation in Emerging Adulthood* (Baker Academic, 2013), 46.

222. Foster, *Celebration of Discipline*, 9.

223. Dallas Willard, *The Kingdom Life: A Practical Theology of Discipleship and Spiritual Formation* (NavPress, 2010), 127.

224. Simon Chan, *Spiritual Theology: A Systematic Study of the Christian Life* (InterVarsity Press, 1998), 191.

225. Chan, *Spiritual Theology*, 191.

226. Chan, *Spiritual Theology*, 191.

227. William Arndt et al., s.v. "δεῖπνον, ου, τό," *A Greek-English Lexicon of the New Testament and Other Early Christian Literature*, 3rd ed. (University of Chicago Press, 2000), 215, Logos.

228. Amanda Brobst-Renaud, "The Great Banquet (Luke 14) and the Church's Great Hunger," *Word & World* 40, no. 1 (Dec. 2020), 18.

229. Brobst-Renaud, "The Great Banquet (Luke 14) and the Church's Great Hunger," 19.

230. Brobst-Renaud, "The Great Banquet (Luke 14) and the Church's Great Hunger," 19.

231. Warren W. Wiersbe, "The Jews: False Security," in *The Bible Exposition Commentary*, vol. 1 (Victor Books, 1996), Luke 14:15-24, Logos.

232. Warren W. Wiersbe, "The Joy of Returning," in *The Bible Exposition Commentary*, vol. 1 (Victor Books, 1996), Luke 15:11-24, Logos.

233. Godwin A. Etukumana, "Prodigality, Repentance and Reconciliation in Luke 15:11-32 and Its Significance to the Family Ethos," in *Neotestamentica* 58, no. 1 (2024) 67, https://doi.org/10.1353/neo.2024.a947411.

234. Anthony Campolo, *The Kingdom of God Is a Party* (Thomas Nelson, 1992), 36.

235. Campolo, *The Kingdom of God Is a Party*, 32.

236. Walter A. Elwell and Philip Wesley Comfort, "Feasts and Festivals of Israel," in *Tyndale Bible Dictionary*, Tyndale Reference Library (Tyndale House Publishers, 2001), 480, Logos.

237. Paul S. Karleen, s.v. "koinonia," *The Handbook to Bible Study: With a Guide to the Scofield Study System* (Oxford University Press, 1987).

238. Agus Setiawan et al., "Coping Mechanisms Utilized by Individuals with Drug Addiction in Overcoming Challenges During the Recovery Process: A Qualitative Meta-synthesis," *Journal of Preventive Medicine & Public Health* 57, no. 3 (May 2024): 8, https://doi.org/10.3961/jpmph.24.042.

239. Byron R. Johnson et al., "Alone on the Inside: The Impact of Social Isolation and Helping Others on AOD Use and Criminal Activity," *Youth & Society* 50, no. 4 (May 2018): 536, https://doi.org/10.1177/0044118X15617400.

240. Johnson et al., "Alone on the Inside," 536.

241. Rosemary Boisvert et al., "Effectiveness of a Peer-support Community in Addiction Recovery: Participation as Intervention," *Occupational Therapy International* (2008): 206.

242. Boisvert et al., "Effectiveness of a Peer-support Community," 206.

243. Christian Scannell, "By Helping Others We Help Ourselves: Insights from Peer Support Workers in Substance Use Recovery," *Advances in Mental Health* (November 2022): 1.

244. Aaron Todd Bicknese, "The Teen Challenge Drug Treatment Program in Comparative Perspective" (PhD diss., Northwestern University, 1999), 3-4, ProQuest.

245. Bicknese, "The Teen Challenge Drug Treatment Program in Comparative Perspective," 23-24.

246. Teen Challenge Southeast Region, "What Is Being Said About Teen Challenge Programs, Megan," https://teenchallenge.cc/reviews/.

247. Irwyn Ince, *The Beautiful Community: Unity, Diversity, and the Church* (InterVarsity Press, 2020), 8, Kindle.

248. Sunhee Kim and Timothy Lim, s.v. "work," *The Lexham Bible Dictionary*, eds. John D. Barry et al. (Lexham Press, 2016), Logos.

249. "Calling and Vocation," Theology of Work Project, https://www.theologyofwork.org/key-topics/vocation-overview -article#toc.

250. "The Businesswoman Lydia (Acts 16)," Theology of Work, https://www.theologyofwork.org/key-topics/women-workers-i n-the-new-testament/the-businesswoman-lydia-acts-16/.

251. Craig S. Keener, *The IVP Bible Background Commentary: New Testament* (IVP, 2014), 370, Kindle.

252. Christopher J. H. Wright, *The Mission of God's People: A Biblical Theology of the Church's Mission* (Zondervan, 2010), 183.

253. Tom Nelson, *The Economics of Neighborly Love: Investing in Your Community's Compassion and Capacity* (IVP Books, 2017), 173.

254. Theology of Work, "Colossians & Philemon and Work," *Theology of Work Bible Commentary,* https://www.theologyofwork.org/new-testament/colossians-philemon/colossians-and-work/heavenly-living-for-earthly-good-the-shape-of-our-reorientation-colossians/.

255. David W. Jones, "From Overwork to Laziness: What Proverbs Tells Us About Work," Center for Faith & Culture, September 10, 2024, https://cfc.sebts.edu/faith-and-work/from-overwork-to-laziness-what-proverbs-tells-us-about-work/.

256. Alistair Mackenzie and Wayne Kirkland, "Everyday Moral Choices," Theology of Work Project, https://www.theologyofwork.org/key-topics/ethics.

257. Bureau of Labor Statistics, "American Time Use Survey-2024 Results," https://www.bls.gov/news.release/pdf/atus.pdf.

258. Richard Bliese, *Eighth Day Discipleship: A New Vision for Faith, Work and Economics* (Eighth Day Discipleship, 2022), 23.

259. William Arndt et al., s.v. "toil," *A Greek-English Lexicon of the New Testament and Other Early Christian Literature*, 3rd ed. (University of Chicago Press, 2000), 558, Logos.

260. Sunhee Kim, s.v. "work," *The Lexham Bible Dictionary* (Lexham Pres, 2016), Logos.

261. Marian V. Liautaud, "Why Our Job Matters: Amy Sherman on Redeeming Work," *Today's Christian Woman*, April 2014, https://www.todayschristianwoman.com/articles/2014/april-week-4/amy-sherman-on-redeeming-work.html.

262. Kyle Idleman, *Gods at War: Defeating the Idols That Battle for Your Heart* (Zondervan, 2013), 2656, Kindle.

263. Wendy Buttacy, *Personal Studies for New Life in Christ* (Adult Teen Challenge USA, 2021), 10.

264. Adult and Teen Challenge, "Recovery Ideas: Reward System," https://teenchallengeusa.org/drug-alcohol-recovery-ideas-reward-system/.

265. Timothy Keller, *Every Good Endeavor* (Random House, 2012), 151, Kindle

266. Keller, *Every Good Endeavor*, 151.

267. "Is Church Work a Higher Calling?" Theology of Work, https://www.theologyofwork.org/key-topics/vocation-overview-article/discerning-gods-guidance-to-a-particular-kind-of-work/church-work-a-higher-calling/.

268. Amy Sherman, "Four Pathways," Vocational Stewardship, https://www.vocationalstewardship.org/pathways/.

269. Kerstin Nilsson, *Designing Sustainable Working Lives and Environments: Work, Health and Leadership in Theory and Practice* (CRC Press, 2024), 178.

270. William Arndt et al., s.v. "Spirit," *A Greek-English Lexicon of the New Testament and Other Early Christian Literature*, 3rd ed. (University of Chicago Press, 2000), 833, Logos.

271. Faithlife, LLC. "Spirit," *Logos Bible Study Bible Sense Lexicon* (Faithlife, 2024), Logos.

272. Roland J. Lowther, "Spirit," in *Lexham Theological Wordbook*, eds. Douglas Mangum et al., Lexham Bible Reference Series (Lexham Press, 2014), Logos.

273. Eugene E. Carpenter and Philip W. Comfort, *Holman Treasury of Key Bible Words: 200 Greek and 200 Hebrew Words Defined and Explained* (Broadman & Holman Publishers, 2000), 400, Logos.

274. Carpenter and Comfort, *Holman Treasury of Key Bible Words*, 400.

275. Jan A. Sigvartsen and James H. Charlesworth, *Afterlife and Resurrection Beliefs in the Pseudepigrapha* (T & T Clark, 2019), 210, Logos.

276. Warren W. Wiersbe, *The Bible Exposition Commentary*, vol. 1 (Victor Books, 1996), John 3:8-13.

277. Edwin A. Blum, "John," in *The Bible Knowledge Commentary: An Exposition of the Scriptures*, eds. J. F. Walvoord and R. B. Zuck (Victor Books, 1985), 2:281, Logos.

278. Walter A. Elwell and Philip Wesley Comfort, *Tyndale Bible Dictionary*, Tyndale Reference Library (Tyndale House Publishers, 2001), 1221-22, Logos.

279. Blum, "John," 2:325.

280. Joel T. Hamme, "Soul," in *Lexham Theological Wordbook*, eds. Douglas Mangum et al., Lexham Bible Reference Series (Lexham Press., 2014), Logos.

281. Hamme, "Soul."

282. Benjamin S. Davis, "Life," in *Lexham Theological Wordbook*, eds. Douglas Mangum et al., Lexham Bible Reference Series (Lexham Press, 2014), Logos.

283. Christopher Wright, *Mission of God: Unlocking the Bible's Grand Narrative* (InterVarsity Press, 2006), 143.

284. David M. Emanuel, "Thinking," in *Lexham Theological Wordbook,* eds. Douglas Mangum et al., Lexham Bible Reference Series (Lexham Press, 2014), Logos.

285. Gerald Cowen, "Mind," in *Holman Illustrated Bible Dictionary*, eds. Chad Brand et al. (Holman Bible Publishers, 2003), 1128, Logos.

286. A. W. Tozer, *The Knowledge of the Holy: The Attributes of God* (Fig, 2017), 47, Kindle.

287. Elwell and Comfort, *Tyndale Bible Dictionary*, 897.

288. Rick Brannan, s.v. "Mind," *Lexham Research Lexicon of the Greek New Testament* (Lexham Press, 2020), Logos.

289. Arndt et al., s.v. "Mind," *A Greek-English Lexicon of the New Testament*, 234.

290. Dallas Willard, *The Kingdom Life: A Practical Theology of Discipleship and Spiritual Formation* (NavPress, 2010), 48.

291. Diane Chandler, *Christian Spiritual Formation: An Integrated Approach for Personal and Relational Wholeness* (Intervarsity Press, 2014), 270.

292. Arndt et al., s.v. "Mind."

293. Martin H. Manser, *Dictionary of Bible Themes: The Accessible and Comprehensive Tool for Topical Studies* (Martin Manser, 2009), Logos.

294. Ryan S. Peterson, "Emotions in the Image of God? The Holistic Vision of Classical Christian Anthropology," *Journal of Spiritual Formation and Soul Care* 16, no. 2 (2023): 203.

295. David Brown et al., *A Commentary, Critical, Experimental, and Practical, on the Old and New Testaments: Matthew–John,* vol. v (William Collins, Sons, & Company, n.d.), Logos.

296. Charlie Self et al., *Life in 5D: A New Vision of Discipleship* (Bronze Bow Publishing, 2022), 85.

297. Angelo Messina, "Mentorship Post-Rehabilitation for Substance Abuse: A Hermeneutic Phenomenological Study" (DHA diss., University of Phoenix, 2024), 71, ProQuest.

298. Jonathon Lookadoo, s.v. "Body," *Lexham Theological Wordbook,* eds. Douglas Mangum et al., Lexham Bible Reference Series (Lexham Press, 2014), Logos.

299. Christian Wolf, s.v. "Body," *Holman Illustrated Bible Dictionary,* eds. by Chad Brand, et al. (Holman Bible Publishers, 2003), 228, Logos.

300. Walter A. Elwell and Philip Wesley Comfort, s.v. "image of God," *Tyndale Bible Dictionary*, Tyndale Reference Library (Tyndale House Publishers, 2001), 230, Logos.

301. Richard Foster, *Prayer: Finding the Heart's True Home* (HarperOne, 2009), 53.

302. Foster, *Prayer*, 53.

303. Foster, *Prayer*, 58.

304. Cathie Macaulay, "The Ignatian Examen: A Contemporary Tool for Awareness and Discernment," (MA thesis, Concordia University, September 2004), 12, https://www.collectionscanada.gc.ca/obj/s4/f2/dsk4/etd/MQ94649.PDF?is_thesis=1&oclc_number=61300605.

305. The Daily Examen, Ignatian Prayer, https://www.ignatianspirituality.com/ignatian-prayer/the-examen/.

306. Richard Foster, *Celebration of Discipline: The Path to Spiritual Growth*, 20th Anniversary ed. (HarperOne, 2018), 27.

307. Foster, *Celebration of Discipline*, 26-27.

308. Alicia Britt Chole, *Ready, Set, Rest: The Practice of Prayer Retreating* (OneWholeWorld, Inc, 2014), 6.

309. Wendy Wood, *Good Habits, Bad Habits: The Science of Making Positive Changes That Stick* (Farrar, Straus, and Giroux, 2019), 10, Kindle.

310. Wood, *Good Habits, Bad Habits*, 12.

311. Diane Chandler, *Christian Spiritual Formation: An Integrated Approach for Personal and Relational Wholeness* (IVP Academic, 2014), 269.

ABOUT THE AUTHOR

Leasa leads the reader alongside biblical figures and their journeys to glean truths for daily living. By using easy to find materials for the creative encounters, she facilitates creative encounters for those who consider themselves artsy and leads the bold non-creatives to trust the process. Leasa, married to her high school sweetheart, has three grown children and seven grandcuties. She is an ordained minister with the Assemblies of God fellowship and holds a Doctorate of Ministry. She is the founder of Restoration Grace, a non-profit based in Oracle, Arizona that promotes spiritual renewal through retreats, workshops and conferences.

www.ingramcontent.com/pod-product-compliance
Lightning Source LLC
Chambersburg PA
CBHW071501140726
47997CB00005B/1810